T0339800

Ecce Homo

&

The Antichrist

Ecce Homo
How One Becomes What One Is

The Antichrist
A Curse on Christianity

Friedrich Nietzsche

In a new Translation by
Thomas Wayne

Algora Publishing
New York

ISBN: 0-87586-281-0 (softcover)
ISBN: 0-87586-282-9 (hardcover)
ISBN: 0-87586-283-7 (ebook)

Library of Congress Cataloging-in-Publication Data

Nietzsche, Friedrich Wilhelm, 1844-1900.
    [Ecce homo. English]
    Ecce homo : how one becomes what one is ; and, The Antichrist : a curse on
Christianity / by Friedrich Nietzsche ; new translations by Thomas Wayne.
      p. cm.
    ISBN 0-87586-281-0 (pbk. : alk. paper) — ISBN 0-87586-282-9 (hard : alk. pa-
per) — ISBN 0-87586-283-7 (ebook)
    1. Nietzsche, Friedrich Wilhelm, 1844-1900. 2. Philosophers—Germany—Bi-
ography. 3. Christianity—Controversial literature. I. Title: Ecce homo : how
one becomes what one is ; and, The Antichrist : a curse on Christianity. II.
Wayne, Thomas. III. Nietzsche, Friedrich Wilhelm, 1844-1900. Antichrist. English. IV. Title: Antichrist. V. Title.

    B3316.N54A3413 2004
    193—dc22
                                    2004006789

Printed in the United States

TABLE OF CONTENTS

TRANSLATOR'S INTRODUCTION

"Nietzsche is the most sarcastic son of a bitch ever to set foot on this earth. Just say that; then write whatever else you want, like he would." — — So my friend Werner Timmermann tells me, with a gleam in his eye. He helped with my translation of *Thus Spake Zarathustra*, a four-year-long labor of love, so he knows what he is talking about. *Zarathustra* (1885) was Nietzsche's magnum opus; everything before it was preparation, everything after it expatiation and elucidation.

But, for some, the question remains: Why Nietzsche? Friedrich Nietzsche (1844-1900) was quite simply one of the most original and influential philosophers who ever lived; in addition, his writing style was brilliant, epigrammatic, idiosyncratic ["It is my ambition to say in ten sentences what everyone else says in a book — what everyone else does *not* say in a book."] The language dances, prances, whirls and twirls; it ranges from ghetto-verbalizations and vulgarizations to high art, from lyricism to sardonicism, from satyr-play to passion play. No one really writes like Nietzsche, though the number of his stylistic apes and imitators is legion (especially in the ranks of academe). Nietzsche, by the way, had nothing but contempt for academics; he considered them sterile mediocrities, puffed-up frogs in need of a pinpricking. So much for professional philosophers and their "definitive" translations of Nietzsche;

their footnotes are good and with one glaring exception (Zarathustra) their translations are even pretty good.

But pretty good is often not good enough when it comes to Nietzsche. In the new translations that comprise this volume, every sentence, every sentiment is prized: every ellipsis, every parenthesis, every italicized phrase and exclamation point is retained as a part and parcel of his literary notation, his philosophical-musical score, if you will. Rhythm and word choice are everything...

This brings us to a second question: Why *The Antichrist* and *Ecce Homo*? Two of this great German's most germane offerings, they were among his last writings. Although he completed them both by the end of 1888, they were considered to be so inflammatory that they were published only years later, in 1895 and 1908, respectively. Both are products of Nietzsche's last creative year. Yet *Ecce Homo* is relatively calm and tranquil, while *The Antichrist* is a jeremiad full of venom and vitriol. The latter is in fact one of the most devastating condemnations of Christianity ever; Nietzsche calls it "the one immortal blemish on mankind," the greatest sin possible against reality, against the spirit of the earth. He goes on to say that "the first and last Christian died on the Cross." His analysis of Jesus and Paul as superlative Jewish types and his portrait of Pontius Pilate as a superior Roman type are thought-provoking, to say the least. One is reminded of Swift's remark from *Gulliver's Travels*: "I cannot but conclude the bulk of your natives to be the most pernicious race of odious little vermin that nature ever suffered to crawl upon the surface of the earth."

That being said, Swift's satire influenced Nietzsche less than Voltaire's skepticism and Schopenhauer's pessimism — Voltaire, whose celebrated phrase with respect to Christianity was "Ecrasez l'infame!" (invoked at the end of *Ecce Homo*); and Schopenhauer, whose comment about religion served as the epigraph for H.L. Mencken's early study of Nietzsche: "I shall be told, I suppose, that my philosophy is comfortless — because I speak the truth; and people prefer to believe that everything the Lord made is good. If you are one such, go to the priests, and leave philosophers in peace."

Nietzsche, of course, rejects metaphysics; he regards God as a crude excuse, an impropriety, an easy way out. In *Ecce Homo* (Behold the man) — the words used by Pilate when he presented Jesus to the Jews — Nietzsche presents us with an autobiographical tour de force, containing not only some of the finest, most incisive and instructive commentary on his own works, but also his singular comments on the "little things," which are, to him, "the fundamental affairs of life itself": nutrition, climate, locality, and recreation. *Ecce Homo* also includes substantial portions of *Zarathustra*, a work for which he has boundless praise, praise which strikes some readers as fulsome and tiresome. Yet when one reflects that he had sold only sixty-some copies in five years, this self-praise is inevitable if not altogether forgivable. On the other hand, Nietzsche claims he wrote the book so as not to get the wrong kind of praise and adulation: "I *desire* no 'believers,' I think I am too malicious even to believe in myself, I never speak to the masses... I have a terrible fear that one day I will be pronounced *holy*: one can guess why I bring out this book *beforehand*, it should prevent them from doing mischief with me... I have no wish to be a saint, I would rather be a buffoon... Perhaps I am a buffoon..."

But, oh! what mischief they have done with him anyway: Nietzsche as precursor, prophet, paragon; Nietzsche the proto-Nazi, poet of the Superman. Take your pick, but be careful which translation/interpretation you read. This leads us to a third question: Why this translation? This version is more faithful than any other, thus, I think, better than any other. Every sentence has been weighed and sifted, sifted and weighed to reproduce Nietzsche's hybrid, high-bred style — that style which encompasses the shrill, strident, sarcastic and bombastic as well as the eloquent, impassioned, refined and resplendent. Nietzsche without tears, then, without scholarly excuses or pretentious "improvements"; Nietzsche without shortcuts; better yet, Nietzsche straight — how odd that sounds! Instead of "prigs" or "bigots," I say "creeps"; instead of "predilection" or "partiality," "preference"; instead of "impudent windmaker," "insolent braggart." And the list goes on: not mistakes, merely missteps, missed rhythms.

Enough, though... At this point I can only point to the remarks of Machado de Assis, the excellent Brazilian novelist: "The best prologue is the one that says the fewest things or which tells them in an obscure or truncated way... The work itself is everything." Indeed.

Thomas Wayne

ECCE HOMO

HOW ONE BECOMES WHAT ONE IS

1

Seeing that shortly I must confront mankind with the heaviest demand ever put on it, it seems to me indispensable to *say who I am*. Basically one should know it: for I have not left myself "unattested." But the disparity between the greatness of my task and the *smallness* of my contemporaries has found expression in the fact that one has neither heard nor even seen me. I live on my own credit, it is perhaps merely a prejudice to say that I am alive?...I need only speak to one of the "cultured people" who come to the Ober-Engadin in the summer to convince myself that I am *not* alive...Under these circumstances it is a duty against which my habit, even more so the pride of my instincts, basically rebels, namely to say: *Hear me! For I am such and such. Above all, do not mistake me for someone else!*

2

I am for example no bugbear at all, no moral monster — I am even the opposite in nature to the kind of man who has hitherto been revered as virtuous. Between you and me, it seems to me that precisely this goes along with my pride. I am a disciple of the philosopher Dionysus, I would rather even be a satyr than a saint. But just read this work. Perhaps I have succeeded, perhaps this work has no other meaning at all than to give expression to this opposition in a cheerful and affable manner. The last thing I would promise would be to "improve" mankind. No new idols will be erected by me; the old may learn what feet of clay they have. *To overthrow idols* (my word for "ideals") — that is more like my calling. Reality has been deprived of its value, its meaning, its truthfulness, to the same degree in which an ideal world has been *fabricated*...The "true world" and the "apparent world" — in plain English: the *fabricated* world and reality...The *lie* of the ideal has hitherto been the curse on reality through which mankind itself has become mendacious and false down to its most basic instincts — to the point of worshipping the *reverse* values of those which alone would guarantee its flourishing, its future, its sublime *right* to a future.

3

He who knows how to breathe the air of my writings knows that it is an air of the heights, a *bracing* air. One must be made for it, otherwise the danger is no small one of catching cold in it. The ice is near, the loneliness is tremendous — but how peacefully all things lie in the light! How freely one breathes! How much one feels *beneath* oneself! Philosophy, as I have understood and lived it hitherto, is the voluntary living among ice and high mountains — the seeking-out of all things curious and questionable in existence, everything that has been put under a ban by morality hitherto. From the long experience afforded me by such a wandering in the *forbidden* I learned to view the first causes for moralizing and idealizing very differently than might be desired: the *secret* history of the philosophers, the psychology of their great names, came to light for me. — How much truth can a spirit *endure*, how much can it *dare*? That became for me more and more the actual measure of value. Error (— the belief in the ideal —)

is not blindness, error is *cowardice...* Every acquisition, every step forward in knowledge *results* from courage, from hardness towards oneself, from cleanliness towards oneself...I do not refute ideals, I simply put gloves on before them...*Nitimur in vetitum:* in this sign my philosophy shall conquer one day, for hitherto they have basically forbidden nothing but the truth. —

4

— Among my writings my *Zarathustra* stands by itself. With this book I have given mankind the greatest gift it has ever been given. This book, with a voice that carries over millennia, is not only the highest book that there is, the true mountain-air book — the whole fact of man lies at a tremendous distance *beneath* it — it is also the *deepest* book, born out of the innermost abundance of truth, an inexhaustible well into which no bucket descends without coming up filled with gold and goodness. Here it is not a "prophet" who speaks, not one of those horrible hybrids of sickness and will to power people call founders of religions. Above all, one must correctly hear the tone that issues from this mouth, this halcyon tone, so as not to do pitiful injustice to the sense of its wisdom. "It is the stillest words that bring on the storm. Thoughts that come on doves' feet rule the world — "

> The figs fall from the trees, they are ripe and sweet; and as they fall their red skin splits open. A north wind am I to ripe figs.
> Thus like figs, my friends, these teachings fall to you: now drink in their juice and sweet flesh! Fall is all around and clear skies and afternoon —

Here no fanatic speaks, here nothing is "preached," here no *belief* is demanded: from an endless abundance of light and depth of happiness falls drop after drop, word after word — the tempo of these speeches is a tender adagio. Such things reach only the most select; it is a privilege without equal to be a listener here; no one is simply free to have ears for Zarathustra...So is Zarathustra not a *seducer*?...But what does he himself say when for the first time he again returns to his solitude? Exactly the opposite of what any "sage," "saint," "world savior" and other *décadent* would say in such a case...He not only speaks differently, he *is* different too...

> Now I go alone, my disciples! You too go away now and alone!
> So I will it!
> Go away from me and protect yourselves against Zarathustra! And better yet: be ashamed of him! Perhaps he has deceived you.
> The man of knowledge must not only love his enemies, he must also be able to hate his friends.
> One repays a tender teacher badly if one always remains a pupil. And why do you refuse to pluck at my wreath?
> You revere me: but what if one day your reverence *comes tumbling down*? Beware lest a statue slay you!
> You say you believe in Zarathustra? But what does Zarathustra matter? You are my believers: but what do all believers matter?
> You had not yet sought yourselves: then you found me. Thus do all believers; therefore all belief means so little.
> Now I bid you lose me and find yourselves; and only *when you have all denied me* will I return to you...
>
> Friedrich Nietzsche

On this perfect day, when everything is ripening and not only the grape is turning brown, a ray of sunshine just fell upon my life: I looked behind me, I looked before me, never have I seen so many and such good things at one time. Not in vain did I bury my forty-fourth year today, I *felt entitled* to bury it — what was vital in it has been saved, is immortal. The first book of the *Revaluation of All Values*, the *Songs of Zarathustra*, *The Twilight of the Idols*, my attempt to philosophize with a hammer — all gifts of this year, even of its last quarter! *How could I not be thankful for my whole life?* — And so I tell myself my life.

WHY I AM SO WISE

1

The good fortune of my existence, its uniqueness perhaps, lies in its fatefulness: I am to express it in the form of a riddle, as my father, already dead, as my mother still alive and growing old. This dual origin, as if derived from the highest and lowest rungs on the ladder of life, at the same time a *décadent* and a *beginning* — this if anything explains that neutrality, that freedom from faction in relation to the total problem of life which perhaps distinguishes me. I have a finer nose for the signs of ascent and descent than any man has ever had, I am the teacher *par excellence* of this — I know both, I am both. — My father died at the age of thirty-six: he was soft, kind, and morbid, like a being destined only to pass by — more a goodly memory of life than life itself. In the same year that his life went on the decline, so did mine: in the thirty-sixth year of my life I reached the lowest point of my vitality — I still lived, but without being able to see three steps in front of me. At that time — it was 1879 — I resigned my Basel professorship, lived through the summer like a shadow in St. Moritz, and the following winter, the most sun-starved of my life, *as a shadow in Naumburg*. This was my low point: "The Wanderer and His Shadow" originated during that time. Undoubtedly I knew about shadows then...In the winter that followed, my first winter in Genoa, that sweetening and spiritualizing which is almost dependent on an extreme poverty of blood and muscle produced "Daybreak." The complete brightness and cheerfulness, even exuberance of spirit, reflected in the said work, is compatible in my case not only with the deepest physiological weakness, but even with an excess of the feeling of pain. In the midst of the torments of an uninterrupted three day brain-pain accompanied by troublesome vomiting of phlegm — I possessed a dialectical clarity *par excellence* and thought very cold-bloodedly through things for which in healthier circumstances I am not enough of a social climber, not cunning enough, not *cold* enough. My readers perhaps know to what extent I regard dialectic as a symptom of decadence, in the most famous case of all, for example: the case of Socrates. — All morbid disturbances of the intellect, even that semi-stupor attendant with fever, have remained to this day alien things to me, about whose nature and frequency I had to first obtain information in a scholarly way. My blood courses slowly. No one has ever been able to confirm fever in me. A doctor who treated me for some time as a nervous case finally said: "No! there is nothing wrong with your nerves, it is simply I myself who am nervous." Absolutely no demonstrable local degeneration of any sort; no organically conditioned stomach complaint, however much of a profound weakness of the gastric system there may be though as a consequence of general exhaustion. Also the eye trouble, at times coming dangerously close to blindness, only an effect, not a cause: so that with every increase in vital strength my strength of vision has also increased again. A long, all too long series of years signifies recovery for me — unfortunately it also signifies at the same time relapse, decline, periods of a kind of *decadence.* After all that, must I say that I am *experienced* in questions of decadence? I have spelled them out forwards and backwards. Even that filigree-art of prehension and comprehension in general, that finger for nuances, that psychology of "seeing round the corner," and whatever else is characteristic of me, was acquired only then, is the true gift of that time in which everything became more refined for me, observation itself together with all the organs of observation. Looking out from a sick perspective toward *healthier* concepts and values, and again conversely, looking down out of the abundance and self-assurance of a *rich* life into the secret working of the instinct of *décadence,* that was my longest exercise, my true experience, if there be any at all in which I became master. I have it now in hand, I have a hand for it, *reversing perspectives*: prime reason why a "revaluation of values" is perhaps possible for me alone.

2

Apart from the fact that I am a *décadent*, I am also the opposite of it. My proof of this, among other things, that I have always chosen the *right* means against bad conditions: while the *décadent* always chooses the means harmful to himself. As *summa summarum*, I was healthy, as an angle, as a specialty, I was *décadent*. That energy for absolute isolation and separation from accustomed circumstances, the self-opposed compulsion to no longer let myself be looked after, waited on, *doctored to* — that betrayed an unconditional instinct of certitude about *what* was needed at that time. I took myself by the hand, I made myself healthy again: the stipulation for this — every physiologist will admit it — is *that one is fundamentally healthy*. A typically morbid being cannot become healthy, nor even less can he make himself healthy; on the other hand, for a typically healthy person being sick can even be an energetic *stimulus* to life, to more life. Thus in fact that long period of sickness *now* seems to me: I discovered life anew, as it were, myself included, I tasted all good and even small things in a way others could not easily taste — I made my philosophy out of my will to health, to *life*...For mark this: it was in the years of my lowest vitality when I *ceased* being a pessimist: the instinct of self-restoration *forbade* me from having a philosophy of destitution and discouragement...And how does one basically recognize *good development*? In that a well-developed man does our senses good: that he is carved from wood which is hard, delicate, and sweet-smelling, all at the same time. He likes only that which is good for him; his preference, his pleasure ceases where the measure of the beneficial is exceeded. He divines remedies against wrongs, he fully utilizes bad incidents to his advantage; what does not kill him makes him stronger. Out of everything he sees, hears, experiences, he instinctively collects *his* sum: he is a selective principle, he rejects much. He is always in *his* society, whether he deals with books, men, or landscapes: he honors in that he *chooses*, in that he *permits*, in that he *intrusts*. He reacts slowly to all types of stimuli, with that slowness which long caution and a willed pride have bred in him — he tests the stimulus which approaches him, he is far from meeting it halfway. He believes neither in "misfortune" nor in "guilt": he comes to terms with himself, with others, he knows how to *forget*, — he is strong enough that to him everything *must* be for the best. — Well then, I am the *opposite* of a *décadent:* for I have just described *myself*.

3

This double set of experiences, this accessibility to seemingly separate worlds repeats itself in my nature in every respect — I am a Doppelganger, I have a "second" face as well as a first. *And* perhaps even a third...Even my origin accords me an outlook beyond all merely local, merely nationally conditioned perspectives, it costs me no trouble to be a "good European." On the other hand, I am perhaps more German than any present-day Germans, Reich Germans, could possibly be — I, the last *anti-political* German. And yet my ancestors were Polish nobility: I have many racial instincts from there in my body, who knows? in the end perhaps even the *liberum veto.* When I think of how often I have been addressed as a Pole while traveling, even by Poles themselves, and how seldom I am taken for a German, then it could appear that German has only been *sprinkled on* me. But my mother, Franziska Oehler, is at any rate, something very German; as is my grandmother on my father's side, Erdmuthe Krause. The latter spent her entire youth in the midst of good old Weimar, not without association with the Goethe circle. Her brother, the Professor of Theology Krause in Koenigsberg, was called to Weimar as General Superintendent after Herder's death. It is not impossible that her mother, my great-grandmother, appears in the diary of the young Goethe under the name "Muthgen." Her second marriage was with Superintendent Nietzsche in Eilenburg; on the day of the great war year 1813 when Napoleon and his general staff entered Eilenburg, on the tenth of October, she had her confinement. As a Saxon, she was a great admirer of Napoleon; it could be that I am one still. My father, born in 1813, died in 1849. Before he took over the pastorship of Roecken, not far from Luetzen, he lived some years at the castle of Altenburg, and instructed the four princesses there. His pupils are now the Queen of Hannover, the Grand Duchess Constantine, the Grand Duchess of Oldenburg, and the Princess Theresa of Saxe-Altenburg. He was full of deep reverence for the Prussian king Frederick William IV, from whom he also received his pastorship; the events of 1848 grieved him beyond measure. I myself, born on the birthday of the said king, on the 15th of October, received, as expected, the Hohenzollern name Friedrich Wilhelm. The choice of the day had at any rate one advantage: throughout my entire childhood my birthday was a holiday. — I consider it a great privilege to have had such a father: it even seems to me that it explains whatever else I possess in the way of privileges — *not* counting life, the great Yea to life. Above all that it requires no intention on my part, but a mere attention, in order to enter involuntarily into a world of higher and gentler things: I am at home there, my innermost passion first becomes free there. That I almost paid for this privilege with my life is certainly no unfair trade. — In order to understand anything at all of my Zarathustra, one must perhaps be similarly qualified as I am — with one foot *beyond* life...

4

I have never understood the art of being prejudiced against myself — this too I owe to my incomparable father — even when it seemed most worthwhile to me. However un-Christian it may seem, I have never once been prejudiced against myself, you may turn my life this way and that, only rarely, basically only once, will you discover any traces of anyone having borne ill-will towards me — perhaps, however, too many traces of *good* will...Even my experiences with those who give everyone a bad time speak without exception in their favor; I tame every bear, I make even the clowns behave. During the seven years when I taught Greek to the senior class at the Basel Academy, I never had occasion to administer punishment; the laziest students were industrious in my company. I am always equal to chance events; I have to be unprepared to be master of myself. Let the instrument be what it will, let the instrument be so out of tune as only the instrument "man" can be — I should have to be sick if I could not manage to coax something worth hearing out of it. And how often have I heard this from the "instruments" themselves, that they had never heard themselves in this way...Most beautifully perhaps from that Heinrich von Stein who died so unpardonably young and who once, after carefully obtaining permission, appeared for three days in Sils-Maria, declaring to everyone that he had *not* come on account of the Engadin. This excellent man, who with all the blustering simplicity of a Prussian Junker had waded into the Wagnerian swamp (— and into that of Duehringism as well!), was as if transformed these three days by a stormwind of freedom, like one suddenly raised to *his* height and given wings. I said to him continually that it was like this for everyone, that one is not 6,000 feet above Bayreuth for nothing — but he refused to believe me...If in spite of that many a small and large misdeed has been done to me, the reason for this was not "the will," least of all *ill*-will: rather indeed could I complain — I have just indicated as much — about the goodwill which has caused no small mischief in my life. My experiences give me a right to a general mistrust of the so-called "selfless" drives, of the whole ready to advise and devise "neighborly love." It strikes me as weakness, as an individual case of the inability to resist stimuli — only among *décadents* is *pity* a virtue. What I cast in the pitying one's teeth is that modesty, reverence, delicacy of feeling easily get lost with them, that pity instantly smells of rabble, that it is the spitting image of bad manners — that under certain circumstances pitying hands can be downright destructive when they reach into a great destiny, into a wounded isolation, into the *privilege* of heavy guilt. The overcoming of pity I reckon among the *noble* virtues: in "Zarathustra's Temptation" I have invented a case where a great cry of distress reaches him, where pity suddenly falls upon him like a final sin and wants to lure him away from *himself*. To remain master here, to keep the *loftiness* of his task pure here of the many baser and more shortsighted impulses which are active in so-called selfless acts, that is the test, the final test perhaps, that a Zarathustra has to pass — his own real *proof* of strength...

5

In still another point I am simply my father once again and as it were his continuation of life after an all-to-early death. Like everyone who has never lived among his equals and to whom the notion of "retaliation" is just as inaccessible as the notion of "equal rights," I forbid myself in cases where a small or a *very great* folly has been committed against me any countermeasure, any protective measure — as is meet, also any defense, any "justification." My kind of retaliation consists in sending after the stupidity some piece of sagacity as quickly as possible: in this way one may yet overtake it. To speak in metaphor: I send a pot of jam to sweeten a *sour* affair...One need only do me wrong, I "repay," of that one may be sure: soon I find an opportunity to express my thanks to the "evildoer" (even for the misdeed, among other things) — or to *ask* him for something, which can be more obliging than giving something...Also it seems to me that the crudest word, the crudest letter is still more good-natured, more respectable than silence. Those who keep silent are almost always lacking in delicacy and courtesy of the heart; silence is an objection, swallowing down necessarily produces a bad character — it even ruins the stomach. All the silent are dyspeptic. — One sees, I do not want crudeness to be undervalued, it is by far the *most humane* form of opposition and, in the midst of modern over-indulgence, one of our foremost virtues. — If one is rich enough for it, it is even a matter of good fortune to be in the wrong. A God come down to earth ought to *do* nothing other than wrong — to take upon himself not the punishment but the *guilt*, that alone would be divine.

6

The freedom from resentment, the enlightenment over resentment — who knows how much I am ultimately obliged in this as well to my long sickness! The problem is not exactly simple: from strength and from weakness one must have experienced it. If anything whatsoever it is to be asserted against being sick, against being weak, it is that in such cases the actual curative instinct, the offense and defense instinct in man grows soft. One does not know how to get free of anything, one does not know how to have done with anything, one does not know how to repulse anything — everything offends. Man and thing come obtrusively near, events strike to deeply, memory is a festering wound. Being sick *is* itself a kind of resentment. — Against this the sick man has but one great remedy — I call it *Russian fatalism*, that fatalism without revolt which the Russian soldier adopts when the campaign becomes too hard for him and he lies down at last in the snow. To no longer accept anything at all, to no longer take anything on, to no longer take anything *in* — to not react at all anymore...The great reason of this fatalism, which is not always simply the courage to die, as life-preserving under the most life-threatening conditions, is in the reduction of the metabolism, its slowing down, a kind of will to hibernation. A few steps further in this logic and one has the fakir who sleeps for weeks in a tomb...Since one would be used up too quickly *if* one reacted at all, one does not even react anymore: this is the logic. And with nothing is one more quickly burned up than with the effects of resentment. Vexation, mortification, morbid susceptibility, the inability for revenge, the lust, the thirst for revenge — for the exhausted one this is surely the most detrimental sort of reaction: it causes rapid consumption of nervous energy, a morbid rise in harmful secretions, bile in the stomach, for example. For the sick person, resentment is the forbidden *in itself* — his evil: unfortunately also his most natural inclination. — That profound psychologist Buddha grasped this. His "religion," which one would do better to define as *hygiene*, to avoid confusing it with such a pitiful thing as Christianity, depended for its effect upon the triumph over resentment: to make the soul free *of it* — first step to recovery. "Not through enmity does enmity come to an end": this stands at the beginning of Buddha's teaching — it is *not* morality that speaks thus, it is physiology that speaks thus. — Resentment, born out of weakness, more harmful to no one more than the weak person himself — in another case, where a rich nature is the prerequisite, an *overflowing* feeling, a feeling that remaining master of is almost the proof of richness. He who knows the earnestness with which my philosophy has taken up the struggle against the feelings of vengefulness and pitifulness right up to the teaching of "free will" — the struggle with Christianity is only a particular instance of it — , will understand why I set forth precisely here my personal procedure, my *sureness of instinct* in terms of practice. In times of *décadence* I forbade them to myself as harmful; as soon as life was rich and proud enough again for them, I forbade them to myself as *beneath* me. That "Russian fatalism" of which I spoke emerged in me this way, that for years I clung tenaciously to almost intolerable situations, localities, habitations, associations, once they were bestowed by chance — it was better than changing them, than *feeling* they were changeable — than rebelling against them oneself...To disturb myself in this fatalism, to be awakened by force at that time I took to be mortally amiss — in fact it was mortally dangerous every time. — To take oneself as a destiny, to not want oneself "different" — in such conditions this is *great reason* itself.

7

War is another thing. I am warlike by nature. To attack is part of my instincts. *To be able* to be an enemy, to be an enemy — perhaps that presupposes a strong nature. It needs resistance, therefore it *seeks* resistance: the *aggressive* pathos belongs just as necessarily to strength as the feelings of vengefulness and pitifulness belong to weakness. Woman, for instance is vengeful: this is a product of her weakness, as is her susceptibility to others' distress. — The strength of the attacker has a sort of *gauge* in the amount of resistance he requires; every increase reveals itself in the seeking out of a powerful opponent — or problem: for a philosopher who is warlike challenges even problems to a duel. The task is *not* to become master over opposition in general, but over those against whom one must pit one's entire strength, flexibility, military mastery — over opponents who are our *equals*...Equality before the enemy — first prerequisite for an *honest* duel. Where one despises, one *can* not wage war; where one commands, where one sees something beneath oneself, one *has* no war to wage. — My practice of war is comprised of four propositions. Firstly: I only attack causes that are victorious — in some cases I wait until they are victorious. Secondly: I only attack causes where I would find no allies, where I stand alone — where I compromise myself alone...I have never taken a single step publicly that did not compromise me: that is *my* criterion for correct action. Thirdly I never attack persons — I only employ the person as a strong magnifying glass with which one can make visible a general but creeping and hardly graspable state of distress. Thus I attacked David Strauss, more precisely the *success* of a decrepit book by the German "culture" — I caught this culture red-handed thereby...Thus I attacked Wagner, more precisely the falsehood, the mongrel instincts of our "culture," which mistakes the artful for the plentiful, the late for the great. Fourthly: I only attack things from which all personal difference is excluded, in which any background of bad experiences is absent. On the contrary, attacking is to me a proof of goodwill, in certain circumstances, of gratitude. I honor a thing, I treat it with distinction by connecting my name with that of a cause, a person: for or against — it is all the same to me. If I wage war against Christianity, it suits me to do so, for I have never experienced any calamities and difficulties from that quarter — the most earnest Christians have always been friendly to me. I myself, an adversary of Christianity *de rigueur*, am far from holding a grudge against the individual for that which is the fate of millennia. —

8

May I venture to point out one last trait of my nature which has caused me no small difficulty in my relations with people? I have an utterly uncanny sensitivity to the instinct of cleanliness, so that I can perceive physiologically — *smell* — the proximity or — what am I saying? — the innermost part, the "innards" of every soul...I have psychological antennae alongside this sensitivity with which I touch and hold every secret in my hand: all the *hidden* filth at the bottom of many a nature, perhaps the product of bad blood but glossed over by education, is already apparent to me almost at first contact. If my observation has been correct, such natures at odds with my sense of cleanliness also feel in their turn the caution of my aversion: this does not make them smell any sweeter...As has always been my custom — extreme cleanliness towards my person is the prerequisite for my existence, I perish under unclean conditions — , I swim and bathe and splash about continually, as it were, in water, in any kind of perfectly transparent and brilliant element. This makes for me no small test of patience in my dealings with men; my humanity consists *not* in sympathizing how man is, but in *enduring* the fact that I do sympathize with him...my humanity is a perpetual self-overcoming. — But I find *solitude* necessary, I mean to say, recovery, return to myself, the breath of a free, light, playful air...My entire Zarathustra is a dithyramb on solitude, or if I have been understood, on *cleanliness*. Fortunately not on *pure folly*. — He who has an eye for color will call it diamond. — *Loathing* for mankind, for "rabble" has always been my greatest danger...Would you like to hear the words in which Zarathustra speaks of the deliverance from loathing?

> But what happened to me? How did I free myself from nausea? Who rejuvenated my sight? How did I fly to the height where rabble no longer sit at the well? Did my nausea itself create wings for me and spring-divining powers?
>
> Verily, to the summit I had to fly to find again the fountain of delight! —
>
> Oh, I found it my brothers! Here at the summit the fountain of delight gushes forth for me! And it is a life in which no rabble can join in and drink!
>
> Almost too furiously you flow for me, spring of delight! And often in wanting to fill it you empty the cup again.
>
> And I must still learn to approach you more demurely: all-too-furiously my heart still flows toward you: —
>
> My heart, upon which my summer burns, short, hot, melancholy, over-happy: how my summer heart yearns for your coolness!
>
> Gone, the lingering misery of my spring! Gone, the snowflakes of my malice in June! Summer have I become entirely and summer-noon, —
>
> — A summer at the summit with cold springs and blissful stillness: O come, my friends, that the stillness may be more blissful still!
>
> For this *our* height and our home: here we live too high and steep for the unclean and their thirst.
>
> You friends, just cast your pure eyes into the fountain of my delight! How could it be troubled by that? It shall laugh back at you with *its* purity.
>
> On the tree Future we build our nest; eagles shall bring us loners food in their beaks!
>
> Verily, no food which the unclean could join in and eat! They would think they were feeding on fire and would burn their mouths.
>
> Verily, no homesteads do we keep ready here for the unclean! An ice-lair our happiness would be to their bodies and to their spirits!
>
> And like strong winds we want to live above them, neighbors to snow, neighbors to the sun: thus do strong winds live.
>
> And like a wind will I one day yet blow among them and take away the breath of their spirit with my spirit: thus my future wills it.
>
> Verily, a strong wind is Zarathustra to all the lower ranks; and with such counsel he counsels all those who spit and spew: beware of spitting *against* the wind!...

WHY I AM SO CLEVER

1

— Why do I know a thing or two *more*? Why am I so clever in general? I have never pondered questions which are not really questions — I have not squandered myself. — I have no experience of actual *religious* difficulties, for example. It escapes me completely as to what extent I should be "sinful." Similarly I lack a reliable criterion for judging pangs of conscience: from what one hears of it, a pang of conscience is not anything respectable...I do not wish to leave an action in the lurch *afterwards*, I would prefer to leave out as a matter of principle the bad outcome, the *consequences*, from the question of value. With a bad outcome one loses far too easily the *correct* eye for what one has done: a pang of conscience seems to me a kind of "evil eye." To honor something that has failed, all the more so *because* it has failed — that goes along much better with my morality. — "God," "immortality of the soul," "redemption," "the next world," all concepts to which I have given no attention, no time either, even as a child — perhaps I was not childish enough for them? I am thoroughly unacquainted with atheism as a result, still less with it as an event: I am too curious, too *incredulous*, too supercilious to put up with a rude and crude answer. God is a rude and crude answer, an indelicacy to us thinkers — , basically even a rude and crude *prohibition* to us: thou shalt not think!...a question which interests me quite differently, upon which the "salvation of mankind" depends more than any theological curiosity: the question of *nutrition*. For everyday use, one may formulate it thus: "How precisely must *you* nourish yourself in order to attain the maximum of strength, of *virtu* in the Renaissance style, of moraline-free virtue?" — Here my experiences have been as bad as they possibly can be; I am astonished to have heard this question so late, to have learned "reason" from these experiences so late. Only the utter worthlessness of our German culture — its "idealism" —

explains to some degree why precisely here I was backward to the point of saintliness. This "culture," which starts off by teaching one to lose sight of realities in order to chase after thoroughly problematical, so-called "ideal" goals, for example, "classical education" — as if it were not already condemned from the start, to unite "classical" and "German" into one concept! Moreover, it is amusing — just imagine a "classically educated" Leipziger! In fact, until I reached my ripest years I only ate *badly* — morally speaking, "impersonally," "selflessly," "altruistically," for the salvation of cooks and other fellow Christians. Thanks to Leipzig cooking, for example, I very seriously denied my "will to life," — at the same time as my first study of Schopenhauer (1865). To ruin one's stomach and still have insufficient nourishment — the aforesaid cooking seems to me to have solved this problem with happy astonishment. (It is said that 1866 brought about a change in this — .) But German cooking in general — what all does it not have on its conscience! Soup *before* the meal (Venetian cookbooks of the sixteenth century still called it *alla tedesca*); over-cooked meat, greasy and mealy vegetables, the degeneration of pastries into paperweights! Add to this the downright bestial post-prandial drinking habits of the ancient and by no means merely the *ancient* Germans, then you can understand the origin of the *German intellect* — in distressed intestines...German intellect is indigestion, it gets finished with nothing. — But the *English* diet as well, which in comparison with the German, even the French diet, is a kind of "return to nature," that is, to cannibalism, goes profoundly against my own instinct; it seems to me that it gives the intellect *heavy* feet — Englishwomen's feet...The best cooking is that of *Piedmont*. — Alcohol does not agree with me; one glass of wine or beer a day completely suffices to make my life a "vale of tears" — in Munich live my antipodes. Granted that I grasped this a little late, I have *experienced* it really since childhood. As a boy I believed wine-drinking to be, like tobacco-smoking, at first but a youthful vanity, later a bad habit. Perhaps the Naumburger wine is partly to blame for this *harsh* judgment. To believe that wine *enlivens* I should have to be a Christian, namely, believe what precisely for me is an absurdity. Strangely enough, along with this extreme ill-humor on account of *small*, strongly diluted doses of alcohol, I am almost like a sailor when it comes to *strong* doses. Already as a boy I showed my bravery in this. To write down and even transcribe a long Latin essay in a single night-watch, with the ambition in my pen to try and emulate my model Sallust in sternness and terseness and pour some grog of the heaviest caliber over my Latin; when I was a student at venerable Schulpforta this was already by no means opposed to my physiology nor perhaps to that of Sallust either — however much it may have been to venerable Schulpforta...Later on, towards the middle of my life, I decided, to be sure, ever more strictly *against* any "spirituous" drinks: I, an opponent of vegetarianism from experience, just like Richard Wagner, who converted me, cannot advise earnestly enough all *more spiritual* natures to absolutely abstain from alcoholic beverages. Water does the job...I prefer places where one can at all times draw water from flowing fountains (Nice, Turin, Sils); a small glass comes with me everywhere I go like a dog. In vino veritas: it appears that here too I am once again at odds with all the world over the concept of "truth" — to me the spirit moves upon the face of the waters...A few more indications of my morality. A hearty meal is easier to digest than one that is too light. The whole stomach working, the first condition for a good digestion. You must know the size of your stomach. For the same reason those lengthy meals which I call interrupted sacrificial feasts are not to be advised, those at the table d'hôte. — No in-between meals, no coffee: coffee spreads gloom. Tea advisable only in the morning. A little, but brisk: tea very detrimental and sicklying over the whole day if it is just a bit too weak. Each person has his own standard here, often between the narrowest and the most delicate limits. In a very agaçante climate it is inadvisable to begin the day with tea: one should start an hour earlier with a cup of thick oil-free cocoa. Sit as little as possible; give credence to no thought that is not born in the open air and accompanied by free movement — in which the muscles do not also celebrate a feast. All prejudices come from the intestines. — Sitting still — I have said it once already — the real *sin* against the holy spirit. —

2

Most closely related with the question of nutrition is the question of *climate* and *locality*. No one is free to live just anywhere; and he who has great tasks to solve which challenge his entire strength has here a very narrow choice indeed. The influence of climate on the *metabolism*, its retardation, its acceleration goes so far that a mistake in climate or locality may not only alienate a person from his task, it can withhold him from it altogether: he never gets a look at it. The animal *vigor* has never become great enough for him to attain that overflowing freedom in the spiritual dimension wherein a person recognizes: *this* I alone can do...An ever so slight inertia of the intestines turned into a bad habit completely suffices to turn a genius into something average, something "German"; the German climate alone is enough to discourage those of strong and even heroically inclined intestines. The *tempo* of the metabolism stands in strict relation with the mobility or lameness of the spirit's *feet*; indeed spirit itself is only a species of this metabolism. List the places where there are or have been intellectual people, where wit, refinement, and malice are part of happiness, where genius is almost necessarily at home: they all have an excellent dry atmosphere. Paris, Provence, Florence, Jerusalem, Athens — these names prove something: genius is *conditioned* by dry air, by pure skies — that means by rapid metabolism, by the possibility of supplying oneself over and over again with large, even enormous amounts of strength. I have in mind a case in which a spirit, freely inclined and of some consequence, became a narrow, withdrawn specialist and sourpuss simply due to a lack of subtle climatic instinct. And I myself might ultimately have arrived at this case had illness not forced me to see reason, to reflect upon reason in reality. Now when from long practice I can read off climatic effects and meteorological origins from myself as if from a very delicate and dependable instrument, and even on a short journey, say, from Turin to Milan, can physiologically verify in myself the change in the degree of humidity, I reflect with horror upon the *ghastly* fact that my life up to the last ten years, the life-threatening years, has always been played out in places false and expressly *forbidden* to me. Naumburg, Schulpforta, Thuringia in general, Leipzig, Basel, Venice — just so many calamity-localities for my physiology. If I have no welcome recollection at all from my entire childhood and youth, then it would be folly here to attribute it to so-called "moral" causes — the indisputable lack of *adequate* company perhaps: for this lack is as present today as ever, but without preventing me from being cheerful and brave. But ignorance *in physiologicis* — accursed "idealism" — has been the real calamity in my life, the superfluous and stupid therein, something from which nothing good can come, for which there is no compensation, no counter-measure. As a consequence of this "idealism" I explain to myself all the blunders, all the great deviations in instinct and "modesties" which diverted me from my *mission* in life, for example, that I became a philologist — why not a doctor at least or something else eye-opening? In my Basel period my whole intellectual regimen, including the arrangement of my day, was an entirely senseless misuse of extraordinary powers, without any sort of covering for the loss of strength, without concern even for loss or compensation. Every finer kind of selfishness was lacking, every *protection* that a domineering instinct provides, it was a setting-oneself-equal with whomever, a "selflessness," a forgetting of one's distance — something for which I will never forgive myself. When I was almost at the end, *because* I was almost at the end, I began to reflect on this basic unreason of my life — "idealism." It was *sickness* that first brought me to reason. —

3

Choice of nutrition; choice of climate and locality; the third thing wherein one may not make a mistake at any price is in *one's kind of recreation*. Here, too, according to the degree to which a spirit is *sui generis*, the limits on what is permitted, what is *useful* are stricter and stricter. In my case all reading is part of my recreation: consequently part of that which lets me get away from myself, going for a stroll among strange sciences and souls — that I no longer take seriously. Reading simply allows me to recover from *my* own seriousness. At deeply laborious times no books are to be seen near me: I would beware of letting anyone talk or even think in my vicinity. And that is what reading really is...Has anyone actually observed that during that profound tension to which pregnancy condemns the spirit and at bottom the whole organism, chance, every kind of outside attraction, acts too vehemently, "strikes" too deeply? Chance, outside attraction, must be avoided as much as possible; a kind of self-immuring is one of the first acts of instinctive shrewdness having to do with spiritual pregnancy. Shall I allow an *alien* thought to climb secretly over the wall? — And that is what reading really is...The periods of labor and fruitfulness are followed by a period of recreation: hither, you pleasant, you witty, you wise books! Shall it be German books?...I have to go back six months before I catch myself with a book in my hand. But what was it? — An excellent study by Victor Brochard, *Les Sceptiques Grecs*, in which my Laertiana are also put to good use. The skeptics, the only honorable sort among that double- to quintuple-dealing tribe of philosophers!...Otherwise I almost always seek refuge in the same books, a small number basically, those books precisely *proven* to me. Perhaps it is not in my nature to read many and many kinds of books: a reading room makes me sick. Nor is it in my nature to love many and many kinds of things. Caution, hostility even, toward new books is rather closer to my instinct than "tolerance," "*largeur du coeur*," and other "good neighborliness"...Basically it is a small number of the older Frenchmen to whom I return again and again: I believe only in French culture and regard everything else in Europe that calls itself "culture" as a misunderstanding, not to mention German culture...The few cases of higher culture that I did come across were all of French extraction, above all Frau Cosima Wagner, by far the foremost voice I have heard in questions of taste.

— That I do not read Pascal but *love* him as the most instructive sacrifice of Christianity, slowly murdered, first physically, then psychologically, the whole logic of this most atrocious form of human cruelty; that I have something of Montaigne's mischievousness in my spirit, who knows? Perhaps also in my body; that my artist's taste takes into safekeeping the names Molière, Corneille, and Racine not without wrath, against a wild genius like Shakespeare: in the end this does not preclude my also finding the most recent Frenchmen to be charming company. I absolutely cannot imagine in which century in history one could haul in such a catch of curious and at the same time delicate psychologists as in present-day Paris: I name, by way of experiment — for this number is by no means small — the Messieurs Paul Bourget, Pierre Loti, Gyp, Meilhac, Anatole France, Jules Lemaître, or, to single out one of a stronger race, a true Latin to whom I am especially attached, Guy de Maupassant. Between ourselves, I prefer *this* generation even to its great masters, all of whom have been altogether ruined by German philosophy (M. Taine, for example, by Hegel whom he has to thank for his misunderstanding of great men and great times). So far as Germany extends, it *ruins* culture. Only the war has "redeemed" spirit in France...Stendhal, one of the most beautiful accidents of my life — for whatever marks an epoch in it came to me by accident, never upon recommendation — is quite invaluable with his anticipatory psychologist eye, with his grasp of fact which closely calls to mind that greatest factual one (*ex ungue Napoleonem* —); last but not least as an *honest* atheist, a scarce and barely ever discoverable species in France — all due respect to *Prosper Merimée*...Perhaps I am even envious of Stendhal? He took away from me the best atheist joke that precisely I could have made: "God's only excuse is that he does not exist"...I myself have said somewhere: what has been the greatest objection to existence thus far? *God*...

4

The highest conception of the lyric poet was given to me by *Heinrich Heine*. I search in vain through all the realms of the millennia for an equally sweet and passionate music. He possessed that divine malice without which I cannot conceive of perfection — I value the worth of a people, of races, according to how necessarily they know not to separate the god from the satyr! It will one day be said that Heine and I have been by far the foremost artists in the German language — at an incalculable distance from all that mere Germans have done with it. — I must be deeply related to *Byron's* Manfred: I have found all these abysses in myself — at the age of thirteen I was ripe for this work. I have no words, only a look, for those who dare to utter the word Faust in the presence of Manfred. The Germans are incapable of every concept of greatness: proof Schumann. Out of anger toward this sugary-sweet Saxon I composed a counter-overture to Manfred, of which Hans von Bülow said that he had never seen the like on music-paper: it was a rope of Euterpe. — When I seek my highest formula for *Shakespeare*, I always find only this, that he conceived of the type of Caesar. Such things cannot be divined — you either are them or you aren't. The great poet draws *only* on his own reality — to the point that afterwards he cannot endure his own work anymore...When I have cast a glance into my Zarathustra I pace back and forth in my room for half an hour, unable to master an insufferable fit of sobbing. — I know of no more heart-rending reading than Shakespeare: what must a man have suffered to have such need of being a buffoon! — Do people *understand* Hamlet? It is *certainty*, not doubt that drives a man crazy...But one must be deep, an abyss, a philosopher in order to feel this way...We are all *afraid* of the truth. And may I confess: I feel instinctively sure and certain that Lord Bacon is the originator, the animal-self-tormentor of this most atrocious kind of literature: what do I care about the pitiful chatter of American muddle- and flatheads? But the strength for the most powerful reality of vision is not only consistent with the most powerful strength of deed, an atrociousness of deed — *it even presupposes it*...We do not know nearly enough about Lord Bacon, the first realist in every large sense of the word, to know *what* all he did, *what* he willed, *what* he experienced in himself...And the hell with my critics! Suppose I had christened my Zarathustra with a name other than my own, for example, with that of Richard Wagner, the acuteness of two-thousand years would not have sufficed to guess that the author of "Human, All-Too-Human" is the visionary of Zarathustra.

5

Here, in speaking of the recreations of my life, I find it necessary to express my gratitude for that which by far has been my deepest and heartiest recreation. This undoubtedly has been my intimate acquaintance with Richard Wagner. I dispense with the rest of my human relations cheaply; at no price would I give away the days of my life spent at Tribschen, days of intimacy, of serenity, of sublime accidents — of *profound* moments...I do not know what others experienced with Wagner: nary a cloud passed over *our* sky. — And with this I come back once again to France — I have reasons, I simply have a contemptuous twist of the mouth for Wagnerians *et hoc genus omne* who think they are doing Wagner an honor by finding him *similar* to themselves...Such as I am, alien in my deepest instincts to all that is German, so that even the nearness of a German retards my digestion, my first contact with Wagner was also the first deep breath of my life: I sensed him, I honored him, as *outland*, as antithesis, as living protest to all "German virtues." — We who were children in the swamp-air of the fifties are of necessity pessimists concerning the concept "German"; we cannot be anything other than revolutionaries — we will not agree to a state of affairs in which a *creep* is on top. It is a matter of complete indifference to me whether he displays other colors today, whether he dresses in scarlet and dons a hussar's uniform...Well then! Wagner was a revolutionary — he ran away from the Germans...As an *artist* one has no home in Europe other than Paris:

the *delicatesse* in all five artistic senses which Wagner's art presupposes, the touch for *nuances*, the psychological morbidity, is found only in Paris. Nowhere else does one have the passionateness in questions of form, this seriousness in *mise en scene* — it is Parisian seriousness *par excellence*. One has absolutely no idea in Germany of the tremendous ambition that dwells in the soul of a Parisian artist. The German is good-natured — Wagner was by no means good-natured...But I have already said enough (in "Beyond Good And Evil": Section 256) about where Wagner belongs, in whom he has his next of kin: it is with the French Late Romantics, that high-flying and still upwardly-rushing species of artists like Delacroix, like Berlioz, with a *fond* of sickness, of incurableness of being, sheer fanatics of *expression*, virtuosos through and through...Who was the first *intelligent* adherent of Wagner, generally speaking? Charles Baudelaire, the same one who first understood Delacroix, that typical *décadent* in whom a whole generation of artists recognized themselves — he was also perhaps the last...What have I never forgiven Wagner? That he *condescended* to the Germans — that he became reichsdeutsch (Imperial German)...So far as Germany extends, it *ruins* culture. —

6

All things considered, I could not have endured my youth without Wagner's music. For I was *condemned* to Germans. If one wants to be free of an unbearable burden, one needs hashish. Well then, I needed Wagner. Wagner is the counter-poison to everything German *par excellence* — poison, I do not dispute it...From the moment there was a piano score of Tristan — my compliments, Herr von Below! — , I was Wagnerian. The earlier works of Wagner I deemed as beneath me — still too common, too "German"...But even to this day I search for a work of equally dangerous fascination, of equally sweet and shuddering infinity as Tristan is — I search in vain in all the arts. All the grotesqueries of Leonardo da Vinci lose their charm at the first note of Tristan. This work is absolutely Wagner's *non plus ultra*; he recuperated from it with the Meistersinger and the Ring. To become healthier — that is a *step backward* for a nature like Wagner's...I take it to be a piece of first-class luck to have lived at the right time and to have lived precisely among Germans, so as to be *ripe* for this work: my psychologist's curiosity goes that far. The world is poor for one who has never been sick enough for this "voluptuousness of hell": it is permissible, it is almost imperative to employ a mystic formula here. — I think I know better than anyone else the enormities Wagner was capable of, the fifty worlds of strange delights, for which no one outside of him had wings; and such as I am, strong enough to turn even the most questionable and dangerous things to my advantage and become stronger thereby, I call Wagner the great benefactor of my life. The manner in which we are related, that we have suffered more deeply, also from each other, than men of this century could possibly suffer, will bring our names together again and again eternally; and as surely as Wagner is merely a misunderstanding among the Germans, so surely I am and will always be. — Two thousand years of psychological and artistic discipline *first*, my dear Teutons!...But that is not easy to make up. —

7

— I still have a word to say for the choicest ears: what *I* actually want from music. That it is cheerful and profound, like an afternoon in October. That it is one of a kind, lively, tender, a sweet little woman of malice and grace...I will never admit that a German *could* know what music is. Those who are called German musicians, the greatest above all, are *foreigners*, Slavs, Croats, Italians, Netherlanders — or Jews: otherwise Germans of a strong race, *extinct* Germans, like Heinrich Schultz, Bach, and Handel. I myself am still enough of a Pole to sacrifice the rest of music in exchange for Chopin; I exempt, for three reasons — Wagner's Siegfried Idyll, perhaps also a few things from Lizst, who excels all other musicians in his noble orchestral tones; finally, all that which has grown up beyond the Alps — *this side*...I could not get by without Rossini, even less without my *South* in music, the music of my Venetian maestro Pietro Gasti. And when I speak of beyond the Alps, I really speak of Venice. When I seek another word for music, I always find only the word Venice. I do not know how to make a distinction between tears and music — I do not know how to think of happiness, of the *South*, without a shudder of fearfulness.

On the bridge I stood
lately in the brown night.
From afar there came a song;
a golden drop, it flowed
across the trembling expanse.
Gondolas, lights, music —
drunken it swam out into the twilight...

My soul, a stringed instrument,
sang to itself, invisibly touched,
a secret gondola song
trembling with iridescent bliss.
— Was anyone listening?

8

In all these things — in the choice of nutrition, of climate and locality, of recreation — an instinct of self-preservation is in command, expressing itself most unambiguously as an instinct of *self-defense*. Not to see many things, not to hear them, not to let them approach one — first act of prudence, first proof for one's being not an accident but a necessity. The customary word for this self-defense instinct is *taste*. Its imperative commands not only to say No when Yes would be an act of "selflessness," but also to *say No as little as possible*. To separate oneself, to detach oneself from that which would necessitate saying No over and over again. The reason in this is that once defensive measures, be they ever so small, become rule, become custom, they involve an extraordinary and completely superfluous impoverishment. Our *large* expenditures are our most frequent small ones. The warding off, the letting things come close is an expenditure — one must not be deluded here — , a *wasted* strength devoted to negative ends. Simply through the perpetual need to ward off, one can become weak enough to no longer be able to defend oneself any longer. — Suppose I were to step out of my house and find, instead of quiet and aristocratic Turin, a German provincial town: my instinct would have to blockade itself in order to push back everything that pressed upon it from this compressed and cowardly world. Or suppose I found a German metropolis, this built-up vice where nothing grows, where everything, good and bad, gets dragged in. Would I not have to become a *hedgehog* over it? — But to have spines is an extravagance, a double luxury even, when one is free not to have spines but *open* hands...

Another act of prudence and self-defense consists in *reacting as seldom as possible* and evading situations and relations where one would be condemned, as it were, to suspend one's "freedom," one's initiative, and become a mere reagent. I take as a metaphor the traffic with books. The scholar, who basically does nothing but "pore over books" — the philologist with a modest daily rate of about two-hundred — utterly loses at last the ability to think for himself. If he doesn't pore, he doesn't think. He *responds* to a stimulus (— a thought he has read) when he thinks — in the end he merely reacts. The scholar relinquishes all his strength in Yea- and Naysaying, in the critique of what has already been thought — he himself thinks no more...The instinct of self-defense has grown rotten in him; otherwise he would defend himself against books. The scholar — a decadent. — I have seen this with my own eyes: gifted, rich and freely-inclined natures already "read to death" in their thirties, mere matches that must be struck in order to have them give off sparks — "thoughts." — Early in the morning at the break of day, in all the freshness and dawn of one's strength, to read a *book* — I call that depraved! — —

9

At this point I can no longer get around giving the proper answer to the question *how one becomes what one is*. And with that I touch on the masterpiece in the art of self-preservation — *selfishness*...For assuming that the task, the destination, the *destiny* of the task is significantly beyond the average measure, then there would be no greater danger than to catch sight of oneself *with* this task. That one becomes what one is presupposes that one does not have the remotest idea *what* one is. From this point of view even life's *blunders* have their own meaning and value, the temporary by-ways and wrong ways, the delays, the "modesties," the seriousness wasted on tasks which lie outside *the* task. Therein a great prudence, perhaps the highest prudence, comes to be expressed: where *nosce te ipsum* would be the recipe for disaster, forgetting oneself, *misunderstanding* oneself, reducing oneself, narrowing oneself, mediocratizing oneself becomes good sense itself. In moral terms: neighborly love, living for others and other things *can* be a protective measure for the maintenance of the most vigorous selfhood. This is the exceptional case in which I take the side of the "selfless" drives, as opposed to my own rule and conviction: here they labor in the service of *selfishness*, of *self-discipline*. — The whole surface of consciousness — consciousness *is* a surface — must be kept clear of any of the great imperatives. Caution even before every grand word, every grand posture! Pure dangers that the instinct will come to "understand itself" too early — . In the meantime the organizing "idea," summoned to rule, is growing and growing in the depths — it begins to command, it slowly leads back out of the by-ways and wrong ways, it prepares individual qualities and abilities beforehand which will prove indispensable as means to a whole — one by one it develops all the serving capacities before any mention of the dominating task, the "goal," the "end," the "meaning." — Viewed from this angle, my life is simply wonderful. For the task of the *revaluation of all values* more capacities were necessary perhaps than have ever dwelt together in one individual: opposing capacities above all as well, except that they were not allowed to disturb or destroy one another. An order of rank among capacities; distance; the act of separating without making an enemy; confusing nothing, "reconciling" nothing; a tremendous multiplicity which is nevertheless the antithesis of chaos — this was the preliminary condition, the long, secret labor and artistry of my instinct. Its *higher protection* was shown to a strong degree by the fact that in no case did I have a presentiment of what was growing in me — that all of my facilities, suddenly ripe, *leapt forth* one day in their final perfection. I fail to remember ever having made an effort — no trace of struggle is detectable in my life, I am the opposite of a heroic nature. To "want" something, to "strive" for something, to have an "end," a "desire" in mind — I know none of this from my experience. Even at this moment I look out upon my future — a *broad* future! — as upon a smooth sea: no desire ripples upon it. Not in the least do I want anything to be different from what it is; I myself do not want to be any different...But thus I have always lived. Not a thing have I wished for. Someone who in his forty-fourth year can say that he has never troubled himself over *honors, women,* or *money!* — Not that I wanted for them...Thus, for example, I one day became a university professor — I had never had the slightest thought about it, for I was hardly twenty-four years old. Thus, two years earlier, I one day became a philologist: in the sense that my *first* philological work, my beginning in every sense, was requested for publication by my master Ritschl in his *Rheinisches Museum* (Ritschl — I say it with reverence — the only scholar of genius my eyes have beheld to this day. He had that pleasant depravity which distinguishes us Thuringians and by which even a German becomes sympathetic — we ourselves prefer the secret by-paths for arriving at the truth. With these words I have no desire whatsoever to undervalue my close countryman, the *intelligent* Leopold von Ranke...).

10

— The question will be asked of me why I actually have brought up these small and, according to traditional judgment, quite insignificant things: I hurt myself thereby, all the more so if I am destined to assume great tasks. Answer: these small things — nutrition, locality, climate, recreation, the entire casuistry of selfishness — are inconceivably more important than everything that has hitherto been considered important. Precisely here one must begin *to learn anew*. Those things which mankind has seriously considered heretofore are not even realities, merely fancies, more strictly speaking, *lies*, arising from the bad instincts of sick, in the deepest sense destructive, natures — all the concepts of "God," "soul," "virtue," "sin," "the beyond," "truth," "eternal life"...But what was sought in them was the greatness of human nature, its "divinity"...All questions of politics, of social organization, of education have been falsified down to the ground and ground-floor because the most destructive men have been taken for great men, because people were taught to despise the "little" things, meaning the fundamental affairs of life itself...If I now compare myself with the men who have heretofore been honored as the *foremost* among men, then the difference is obvious. I do not even count these alleged "foremost ones" as men in general — to me they are the refuse of humanity, products of sickness and vengeful instincts: they are absolutely pernicious, fundamentally incurable monsters taking their revenge upon life...I want to be the opposite of this: it is my privilege to have the highest acuteness with respect to all the signs of healthy instincts. Every morbid trait is lacking in me; even in times of serious illness I did not become morbid; one would look in vain for any trait of fanaticism in my character. At no moment in my life could one point to any arrogant or pathetic posturing on my part. The pathos of poses does *not* belong to greatness; he who needs poses is *false*...Beware of all picturesque men! — Life always became easy for me, easiest, when it demanded the hardest things from me. Whoever saw me during the seventy days this fall when, without interruption, I produced nothing but first-rate things which no man could do after me — or before me, with a responsibility to all the coming millennia, will have noticed no trace of tension in me, but rather an overflowing freshness and cheerfulness. I never ate with greater gusto, I never slept better. — I know of no other way of dealing with tasks than *play*: this is, as a sign of greatness, an essential prerequisite. The least constraint, a gloomy mien, any harsh note in the voice, all are objections against a man, and how much more so against his work!...One must have no nerves...Also to suffer from solitude is an objection — I have always suffered from the "multitude"...At the absurdly early age of seven I already knew that no human speech would reach me: has anyone ever seen me sad on that account? — Today I still have the same affability toward everybody, I am even full of respect for the lowliest: in all this there is not a grain of haughtiness, of secret contempt. He whom I despise *divines* that he is despised by me: through my mere existence I enrage all those who have bad blood in their veins...My formula for human greatness is *amor fati*: that one wants nothing to be different, not in the future, not in the past, not for all eternity. Not only to endure what is necessary, still less to conceal it — all idealism is falseness in the face of necessity — , but to *love* it...

WHY I WRITE SUCH GOOD BOOKS

1

I am one thing, my writings are another. — Here, before I speak of these writings themselves, I will touch upon the question of their being understood or *not* being understood. I do it as casually as is somehow fitting: for the time has not yet come at all for this question.

My time has not yet come, some people are born posthumously. — At some time or other, institutions will be required in which people live and teach the way I understand living and teaching: perhaps individual academic chairs will also be set up for them for the interpretation of Zarathustra. But it would be a complete contradiction of myself were I to already expect ears *and hands* for *my* truths today: that no one hears me today, that no one knows how to take me today, is not only understandable, it even seems the right thing to me. I do not want to be mistaken for someone else — that also means that I do not mistake myself for someone else. — To say it once more, there is very little proof in my life of "ill-will"; of literary "ill-will" as well I would hardly know of a single case to relate. On the contrary, too much *pure folly*!...It seems to me that to take up one of my books in hand is one of the rarest distinctions a person can bestow upon himself — I take for granted that he also takes his shoes off — not to mention his boots...When Doctor Heinrich von Stein once honestly complained about not understanding a single word of my Zarathustra, I said to him that that was as it should be: to have understood six sentences from it, that to have *lived* them, raises one to a higher plane of the mortal than "modern" men could attain. How could I, with this feeling of distance, ever desire to be read by those whom I know — the "moderns"! — My triumph is exactly the reverse of Schopenhauer's — I say "*non* legor, non legar." — Not that I should like to underestimate the pleasure afforded me more than once by the *innocence* in which No is expressed toward my writings. This very summer yet, at a time when I could possibly upset the balance of the whole rest of literature with my weighty, so very weighty literature, a professor of Berlin University kindly gave me to understand that I really ought to use another form: nobody could read such things. — In the end it was not Germany but Switzerland that presented me with the two extreme cases. An essay by Dr. V. Widmann on *Beyond Good And Evil* in the *Bund*, under the title "Nietzsche's Dangerous Book," and a collective report about my works in general on the part of Herr Karl Spitteler, likewise in the *Bund*, represent a high point in my life — I hesitate to say of what...The latter, for example, dealt with my Zarathustra as a higher exercise in style, with the wish that later on I might try to provide some content as well; Dr. Widmann expressed his respect for the courage with which I strove to abolish all decent feelings. — Through a little trick of fate, every sentence here was, with a logical consistency I had to admire, a truth stood on its head: one basically had to do nothing more than "revalue all values" in order to hit the nail on the head with me in a very noteworthy way — instead of hitting my head with a nail...I try to find an explanation all the more. — In the end, no one can "hear" more out of things, books included, than he already knows. Whatever one has no access to through experience one has no ears for. Now let us imagine an extreme case: that a book speaks of nothing but events which lie entirely outside the possibility of a frequent or even rare experience — that it is the *first* utterance for a new range of experiences. In this case simply nothing will be heard, along with the acoustical delusion that where nothing is heard *there is nothing there either*...This is, in the end, my average experience and, if you will, the *originality* of my experience. Whoever believed he had understood something of me had made me up out of me something after his own image — not infrequently the antithesis of me, for instance, an "idealist"; whoever had understood nothing of me denied me any consideration whatsoever. — The word "Superman" as the designation for a type of the highest successfulness as opposed to "modern" men, to "good" men, to Christians and other nihilists — a word that in the mouth of a Zarathustra, the *annihilation* of morality, becomes a very thought-provoking word — has been understood almost everywhere with complete innocence in the sense of those values whose antithesis the figure of Zarathustra was meant to represent: that is to say, as the "idealistic" type of a higher kind of man, half-"saint," half-"genius"...Other learned dolts have suspected me of Darwinism on that account; even the "hero-worship" of that great unwilling and unknowing swindler Carlyle, which I maliciously dismissed, was recognized in it. Whosoever's ears I whispered into that he had better look around for a Cesare Borgia rather than a

Parsifal would not believe his ears. — That I am without any curiosity about reviews of my books, especially in the newspapers, will have to be forgiven me. My friends, my publishers, know this and do not speak to me of such things. In one particular case I once came to see all the sins that were committed against a single book — it was "Beyond Good and Evil"; I could tell a nice story about that. Would you believe that the "Nationalzeitung" — a Prussian newspaper, as I note for my foreign readers — I myself read, with your permission, only the Journal des Debâts — could in all seriousness see the book as a "sign of the times," as the true-blue Junker philosophy, for which the Kreuzzeitung simply lacked the nerve?...

2

This was said for Germans: for everywhere else I have readers — none other than *choice* intelligences, tried and tested in high positions and duties; I even have actual geniuses among my readers. In Vienna, in St. Petersburg, in Stockholm, in Copenhagen, in Paris and New York — everywhere I have been discovered: *not* in Europe's flatland Germany. And to confess it, I rejoice even more over my non-readers, those who have heard neither my name nor a word of my philosophy; but wherever I go, here in Turin for instance, every face becomes bright and right at the sight of me. What has flattered me most thus far is that old market-women cannot rest easy until they have picked out the sweetest of their grapes for me. *To this extent* one must be a philosopher...The Poles are not called the French among the Slavs for nothing. A charming Russian lady would not mistake for a moment where I belong. I cannot be solemn, the best I can do is appear embarrassed. To think German, to feel German — I can do anything, but *that* is beyond my powers...My old master, Ritschl, even maintained that I conceived my very philological treatises like a Parisian *romancier* — absurdly exciting. In Paris itself they are astounded over "*toutes mes audaces et finesses*" — the expression is from Monsieur Taine — : I fear that even into the highest forms of the dithyramb one will find in me an admixture of that salt which never goes flat — goes "German" — *esprit* (that is what I mean)...I cannot do otherwise. So help me God. Amen. — We all know, some of us even know it from experience, what a long-ears is. Well then, I dare to assent that I have the smallest ears. This interests the ladies not just a little — it seems to me they feel themselves better understood by me?...I am the *anti-ass* par excellence and with that a world-historical monster — I am, in Greek and not only in Greek, the *Antichrist*...

3

I pretty well know my privileges as a writer; in some cases it has even been made plain to me how much getting used to my writings "spoils" one's taste. One simply cannot stand other books, least of all, philosophical books. It is a distinction without equal to enter this noble and subtle world — one must absolutely not be a German; it is in the end a distinction one must have earned. He, however, who is related to me through *loftiness* of will experiences true ecstasies of learning thereby: for I come from heights to which no bird has ever flown, I know abysses into which no foot has ever gone astray. People have told me that once they begin it is impossible to put down a book of mine — I even disturb a peaceful night's sleep...There is absolutely no prouder and at the same time more refined kind of book than mine are — they attain here and there the highest that can be attained on earth, namely, cynicism; even so, to conquer them one must have the softest fingers as well as the bravest fists. Every infirmity of the soul excludes one from them, once and for all, every form of dyspepsia: one must have no nerves, one must have a joyful belly. Not only the poverty, the crooked air of a soul excludes one, even more so the cowardly, the unclean, the secret vengefulness in the innards: a word from me brings all these bad instincts to the surface. I have among my acquaintances many guinea pigs through whom is brought home to me the various, very instructive-rich various, reactions to my writings. Those who want to have nothing to do with their contest, my so-called friends, for example, become "impersonal": they congratulate me on "pulling it off" again — and give out that progress has been made in a greater cheerfulness of tone...The utterly depraved "spirits," the "beautiful souls," the thoroughly and completely untruthful ones have no idea at all where to begin with these books — consequently they see the same as beneath them, with the beautiful logical consistency of all "beautiful souls." The dolts among my acquaintances, mere Germans if I may say so, have given me to understand that they are not always of my opinion, but nevertheless now and then...I have heard this about my Zarathustra...Likewise all "feminism" in people, in men as well, a shutting of the gates to me: one will never enter this labyrinth of daring perceptions. One must never have spared oneself, one must have *hardness* in his habits, to be good-humored and gay among nothing but harsh truths. When I make a mental image of the perfect reader, it always turns out to be a monster of courage and curiosity, not to mention someone supple, wily, wary, a born adventurer and discoverer. Finally: I would not know how to say better to whom alone I basically speak than Zarathustra has said it: *to whom* alone will he reveal his riddle?

> To you, the daring searchers, researchers,
> and whoever has set sail with subtle sails on
> frightful seas, —
> To you, the riddle-intoxicated,
> the twilight delighted, whose souls
> are lured by flutes to every mis-abyss:
> — For you refuse to grope along a
> thread with a cowardly hand; and
> where you can *divine* you hate to deduce...

4

At the same time I want to say a word in general about my *art of style*. To *communicate* a state, an inner tension of pathos through signs, including the tempo of these signs — that is the point of every style; and considering that in my case the multiplicity of inner states is extraordinary, there exist many stylistic possibilities for me — the most manifold art of style upon the whole than any man has ever had at is disposal. Any style is good which actually communicates an inner state, which makes no mistake over the signs, over the tempo of the signs, over *gestures* — all laws of phrasing belong to the art of gestures. Here my instinct is infallible. — Good style *in itself* — a pure piece of folly, mere "idealism," of a piece with the "beautiful *in itself*," the "good *in itself*," the "thing in itself"...Still presupposing that there are ears — that there are those capable and worthy of the same feeling, that there is no lack of those to whom one *may* communicate oneself. — My Zarathustra, for example, is still looking for such as those the while — alas! he will still have to look for a long time! — One must be *worthy* of trying him out...And until then there will be no one who grasps the *art* that has been wasted here: no one has ever had artistic means to waste which were so new, so unheard of, and so expressly designed only for that purpose. That precisely such a thing was possible in the German language remained to be seen: I myself would have rejected it most harshly beforehand. Before me no one knew what could be done with the German language — what could be done with the language in general. The art of the *grand* rhythm, the *grand style* of periodic, as the expression of the tremendous up and down of sublime, of superhuman passion, was first discovered by me; with a dithyramb like the last one in the *third* part of Zarathustra, entitled "The Seven Seals." I flew a thousand miles beyond that which was hitherto called poesy.

5

— That out of my writings a *psychologist* without equal speaks, that is perhaps the first insight a good reader makes — a reader such as I deserve, who reads me the way old philologists read their Horace.

The propositions over which the whole world is fundamentally in agreement — not to mention at all everyone's favorite philosophers, moralists, and other jugheads, cabbage heads — appear to me as naïve blunders: for example, the belief that "unegoistic" and "egoistic" are opposites, while the ego itself is merely a "higher swindle," an "ideal"...There are *neither* egoistic *nor* unegoistic acts: both concepts are psychological nonsense. Or the proposition that "man strives for happiness"...Or the proposition that "happiness is the reward of virtue"...Or the proposition that "pleasure and pain are opposites"...Morality, the Circe of humanity, has utterly falsified *all psychologica* — "*demoralized*" them — down to that frightful nonsense that love is supposed to be something "unegoistic"...One must be firmly set with *oneself*, one must stand bravely upon one's own two feet, otherwise one *cannot* love at all. In the end the little women know that all too well: They don't give a hoot in hell about selfless, merely objective men...May I venture the conjecture, by the way, that I *know* women? That is part of my Dionysian inheritance. Who knows? Perhaps I am the first psychologist of the eternal-feminine. They all love me — an old story: with the exception of the *failed* women, the "emancipated" ones unable to have children. — Fortunately I am not willing to have myself torn to pieces: the perfect female tears to pieces when she loves...I know these amiable Maenads...Ah, what a dangerous, creeping, subterranean little beast of prey she is! And so agreeable at the same time!...A little woman, bent on revenge, would run over destiny itself. — Woman is unspeakably more evil than man, more clever also; goodness in a woman is already a form of *degeneration*...All so-called "beautiful souls" have a physiological ill as their basis — I do not say all there is to say, lest I become medi-cynical. The struggle for *equal* rights is in fact a symptom of illness: every doctor knows this. The more womanly a woman is, the more she fights tooth and nail against rights in general: the natural state of things, the eternal *war* between the sexes, certainly assigns her by far the first rank. — Has anyone heard my definition of love? It is the only one worthy of a philosopher. Love — in its means, war, in its basis, the deadly hatred between the sexes. — Has anyone heard my answer to the question how a woman is *cured* — "saved"? One produces a child for her. A woman needs children, the man is always only a means: thus spake Zarathustra. — "Emancipation of women" — this is the instinctive hatred of the *dysfunctional*, that is, unfruitful woman, toward one who is functional — the struggle against "man" is always only a means, a pretext, a tactic. By elevating *themselves* as "woman per se," as "higher woman," as woman "idealist," they want to bring *down* the general rank and level of women; there is no surer means for that than higher education, trousers, and political voting-cattle rights. Basically, the emancipated are the *anarchists* in the world of the "eternal feminine," those who have missed the boat and whose deepest instinct is for revenge...A whole species of the most malevolent "idealism" — which, by the way, also occurs in men, for instance in Henrik Ibsen, that typical old maid — has as its goal the poisoning of good conscience, of the natural love between the sexes...And so as to leave no doubt concerning my honest as well as strict conviction in this matter, I will yet impart a clause from my moral codex against *vice*: with the word vice I take arms against every kind of anti-nature, or if you prefer fine words, every kind of idealism. The clause reads: "The preaching of chastity is a public incitement to anti-nature. All despisal of the sex life, all defiling of the same through the concept of "unclean" is the very crime against life — is the actual sin against the holy spirit of life." —

6

To give some idea of me as a psychologist, I take a curious piece of psychology which appears in "Beyond Good And Evil," — in passing, I forbid any conjecture about whom I may be describing in this passage. "The genius of the heart, as that great mysterious one possesses it, the tempter-god and born rat-catcher of consciences, whose voice knows how to descend to the netherworld of every soul, who says not a word nor casts a glance in which there might not be a note and notice of allurement, whose mastery includes knowing how to appear — not as he is, but as one constraint for those who follow him to crowd themselves ever closer upon him, to follow him ever more inwardly and profoundly...The genius of the heart, who imposes silence and obedience on everything loud and self-conceited, who smooths out the rough souls and makes them taste a new longing — to lie still, like a mirror, that the deep heavens may be reflected in them...The genius of the heart, who teaches the clumsy and overhasty hand to tarry and grasp more delicately; who divines the hidden and forgotten treasure, the drops of goodness and sweet spirituality under the thick dark ice, and is a divining rod for every speck of gold long buried in the dungeon of much mud and sand...The genius of the heart, from whose touch everyone goes away richer, not divinely favored and taken by surprise, not blessed and oppressed by an alien commodity, but richer in oneself, newer to oneself than before, broken loose, blown upon and sounded at by a thawing wind, more uncertain perhaps, more breakable, more brittle, more broken, but full of a new will and current, full of a new ill-will and counter-current...

THE BIRTH OF TRAGEDY

1

In order to be fair to "The Birth Of Tragedy" (1872) a few things will have to be forgotten. Where it failed it also *achieved its effect* and even fascinated — with its practical application to *Wagnerism*, as if the latter were a symptom of ascent. Even with that his essay was an event in Wagner's life: from then on there were high hopes associated with the name Wagner. Even today I am reminded of it, possibly in connection with Parsifal: how I am actually the one morally responsible for the fact that such a high opinion of the *cultural values* of this movement has come to prevail. More than once I found the book referred to as "The Re-birth of Tragedy out of the Spirit of Music": people only had ears for a new formula for *Wagner's* art, aim, mission — what was of hidden yet fundamental value was thus overlooked in the book. "Hellenism and Pessimism": that would have been an unambiguous title: namely as the first lecture on how the Greeks managed their pessimism — how they *overcame* it...Tragedy is precisely the proof that the Greeks were *not* pessimists: Schopenhauer was in error here, as he was in error everywhere. Viewed with some neutrality, "The Birth of Tragedy" appears very untimely: no one would ever dream that it was *begun* amid the thunder of the battle of Woerth. I thought through these problems on cold September nights beneath the walls of Metz, while on duty as a medical orderly; one would much sooner believe that the work was fifty years older. It is politically indifferent — "un-German," one would say nowadays — , it smells offensively Hegelian, only a few formulas are infected with that old person at a funeral smell of Schopenhauer. An idea — the Dionysian/Apollonian antithesis — translated into metaphysics; history itself as the development of this "idea"; in tragedy this antithesis sublimated into a unity; from this perspective, things which had never faced each other before suddenly juxtaposed, illuminating and *clarifying* each other...opera, for example, and revolution...The two decisive *innovations* are firstly, the comprehension of the *Dionysian* phenomenon among the Greeks — it presents the first psychology of this phenomenon, it sees in the latter the one root in the whole of Greek art — . Secondly is the comprehension of Socratism: Socrates recognized for the first time as the tool of Greek dissolution, as the typical *décadent*. Reason *versus* instinct. "Reason" at any price as a dangerous, as a life-undermining force! — A deeply hostile silence toward Christianity throughout the book. Christianity is neither Apollonian nor Dionysian; it *negates* all *aesthetic* values — the only values acknowledged by "The Birth Of Tragedy": it is in the deepest sense *nihilistic*, whereas in the Dionysian symbol the utmost limit of *affirmation* is attained. At one point the Christian priesthood is alluded to as a "malicious species of dwarves" of "underground ones"...

2

This beginning is remarkable beyond all measure. I had discovered the only parable and parallel that history has to my own innermost experience — and so with that I was the first to grasp the wonderful phenomenon of the Dionysian. At the same time, by my recognizing Socrates as a *décadent*, I gave a completely unequivocal proof how little danger the sureness of my psychological grasp would encounter at the hands of some moral idiosyncrasy — to see morality itself as a symptom of decadence is an innovation, a unique event of the first order in the history of knowledge. How high I had leaped with both above and away from the wretched flathead-chatter of optimism *versus* pessimism! — I was the first to see the essential contrast — the *degenerative* instinct, which turns itself against life with a subterranean vengefulness (— Christianity, the philosophy of Schopenhauer, in a certain sense even the philosophy of Plato, all idealism in its typical forms), as opposed to a formula of the *highest affirmation*, one born out of abundance, out of superabundance, a Yea-saying without reserve to suffering itself, to guilt itself, to everything questionable and alien in existence itself...This final, most joyful, most excessively-exuberant yes to life is not only the highest insight, it is also the *deepest*, the one most strictly confirmed and supported by truth and science. Nothing is to be neglected, nothing is to be dispensed with — those aspects of life which Christians and other nihilists reject are of an even higher order in the ranking order of values than those which the *décadence*-instinct might think good and *call good*. To grasp this requires *courage* and, as a condition of that, an excess of *strength*: for exactly as far as courage *dares* to venture forward, exactly to that degree one approaches the truth. Knowledge, the yea-saying to reality is just as much a necessity to the strong as cowardice and the *flight* from reality — the "ideal" — is to the weak, inspired by weakness...They are not free to perceive: decadents find the lie *necessary* — it is one of their conditions of self-preservation. — He who not only understands the word "Dionysian" but understands *himself* in the word "Dionysian" needs no refutation of Plato or Christianity — he *smells the putrefaction...*

3

To what extent I discovered the concept of "tragic" and with it precisely the final knowledge about the psychology of tragedy I have last expressed in *The Twilight Of The Idols*: "The yea-saying to life, even to its strangest and hardest problems; the will to life, rejoicing over its own inexhaustibility in the sacrifice of its highest types — *that* is what I called Dionysian, that is what I understood as the bridge to the psychology of the *tragic* poet. *Not* to be free of fear and pity, not to purge oneself of a dangerous emotion through a vehement discharge — thus Aristotle misunderstood it — : but to be above and beyond fear and pity, *to be oneself* the eternal joy of Becoming itself — that joy which also includes the *joy in destroying...*"In this sense I have the right to regard myself as the first *tragic philosopher* — that is to say, the ultimate antithesis and antipode to a pessimistic philosopher. Before me this transposition of the Dionysian into a philosophical pathos did not exist: the *tragic wisdom* was absent — I have searched in vain for signs of it even among the *great* Greek philosophers, those who lived in the two centuries *before* Socrates. I still had some doubt about *Heraclitus*, in whose presence I feel warmer and happier in general than anywhere else. The affirmation of flux *and destruction*, the decisive element in a Dionysian philosophy, the yea-saying to contradiction and strife, the notion of *Becoming*, along with the radical rejection of even the concept, "Being" — therein I am forced to recognize in any event that which is closest to me of all that has previously been thought. The doctrine of the "Eternal Recurrence," that is, of the unconditional and endlessly repeating circulation of all things — this doctrine of Zarathustra's *could* possibly in the end also have been taught by Heraclitus. At least the Stoics, who derived all their fundamental ideas from Heraclitus, possessed traces of it.

4

Out of this book speaks a tremendous hope. In the end I lack every reason for taking back the hope of a Dionysian future for music. Let us look a century ahead, let us suppose that my attempt on two thousand years of anti-nature and human defilement were to succeed. That new party of life, which would take up the greatest of all tasks, the higher breeding of mankind, including the pitiless annihilation of all degenerates and parasites, will make possible again that *excess of life* on earth from which the Dionysian condition must rise again as well. I give promise of a *tragic* age: the highest art in life affirmation, the tragedy, will be reborn when mankind has put behind it the consciousness of the hardest but most necessary wars *without suffering from it*...A psychologist might yet add that what I heard of Wagner's music had nothing whatsoever to do with Wagner; that when I described Dionysian music I described *that* which *I* had heard — that instinctively I had to translate and transfigure everything into the new spirit I carried within me. The proof for that, *as strong as any proof can be*, is my essay "Wagner in Bayreuth": in all the psychologically decisive passages the conversation is only about me — one may unhesitantly put down my name or the word "Zarathustra" wherever the text has the word Wagner. The whole picture of the *dithyrambic* artist is a picture of the *pre-existent* poet of Zarathustra, sketched with abysmal profundity and without even touching for a moment on the Wagnerian reality. Wagner himself had an inkling of this; he did not recognize himself in the essay. In the same way "the idea of Bayreuth" was transformed into something which may not be a puzzling idea to those who know my Zarathustra: into that *great noontide*, when the most select ones dedicate themselves to the greatest of all tasks — who knows? The vision of a festival which I will yet live to see...The pathos of the first pages is world-historical; the *look* spoken of on page seven is the true Zarathustra-look; Wagner, Bayreuth, the whole little German miserableness is a cloud in which an endless fata morgana of the future is reflected. Even psychologically all the decisive traits of my own character enter into that of Wagner — the juxtaposition of the most luminous and most ominous forces, the will to power as no man has ever possessed it before, the reckless bravery in matters of the spirit, the boundless strength to learn without the will to action being crushed by it. Everything in this essay is prophetic: the imminent return of the Greek spirit, the necessity of *counter-Alexanders* who will retie the Gordian knot of Greek culture after it has been cut...Listen to the world-historical accent with which (in section 4) the concept of "tragic disposition" is introduced: there is nothing but world-historical accents in this essay. This is the oddest "objectivity" there can be: the absolute certainty over what I *am* has projected itself onto ant casual reality — the truth about me speaks from a dreadful depth. (In section 9) the *style* of Zarathustra is described and anticipated with incisive certainty; and never will one find a more magnificent expression of the Zarathustra *event*, the act of a tremendous purification and consecration of mankind's, than is found (in section 6). —

THE UNTIMELY ESSAYS

The four *untimely* essays are thoroughly warlike. They prove that I was no John-a-dreams, that it gives me pleasure to draw the sword — perhaps also that I am dangerously quick on the draw. The *first* attack (1873) was directed at German culture, which even at that time I looked down upon with pitiless contempt. Without sense, without substance, without scope: "simply public opinion." There is no more vicious misunderstanding than to believe that the great military success of the Germans proved anything in favor of this culture — or, of all things, *its* triumph over France...The *second* untimely essay (1874) throws light on the dangerous life-corroding and life-poisoning in our method of scientific pursuit — : life *sick* on account of this inhuman machinery and mechanism, this "*im*personality" of the worker, this false economy of the "division of labor." The aim is lost, the culture — the means of modern scientific pursuit, *barbarized*...In this essay the "historical sense," of which this century is so proud, is recognized as a typical sign of decay. — In the *third* and *fourth* untimely essays two pictures of the harshest *self-connection, self-correction* are set up as signs pointing the way to a higher concept of culture, to a restoration of the concept of "culture" — untimely types *par excellence*, full of sovereign contempt for everything around them with the name "Reich," "Culture," "Christianity," "Bismarck," "Success" — Schopenhauer and Wagner or, in a word, Nietzsche?

2

Of these four assassination attempts the first had an extraordinary success. The uproar it evoked was in every sense magnificent. I had touched a victorious nation on its sore spot — that its victory was *not* a cultural event, but perhaps, perhaps something quite different...The reply came from all sides and by no means simply by the old friends of David Strauss, whom I had made fun of as the type of a German culture-philistine and *satisfait*, in short, as the author of that alehouse gospel of "old and new faith" (the term Bildungsphilister has remained in the language since the time of my essay). Those old friends, Wuertembergers and Swabians whom I had stung deeply when I found their prodigy, their Strauss comical, replied as loyally and rudely as I could possibly have desired; the Prussian responses were shrewder — they had more "Berliner Blue" in them. A Leipziger newspaper, the infamous "Grenzboten," provided the most indecent response; I had a hard time restraining the enraged Baselers from taking action against it. Only a few old gentlemen were unconditionally decided in my favor, out of mixed and in part out of undiscoverable motives. Among them Ewald in Goettingen, who intimated that my attempt proved quite fatal to Strauss. Likewise the old Hegelian Bruno Bauer, who was henceforth one of my most attentive readers. In his later years he loved to refer to me when giving a hint to Heinrich von Treitschke, for example, the Prussian historiographer, as to where he (von Treitschke) might find information about the concept of "culture" which had eluded him. The longest and most thoughtful response to the essay was that of an old pupil of the philosopher von Baader, a Professor Hoffman in Wuerzburg. From the essay he foresaw a great destiny for me — to bring about a kind of crisis and utmost decision in the problem of atheism, the most instinctive and ruthless type of which he divined in me. It was atheism that led me to Schopenhauer. — Best heard by far and most bitterly felt was an extraordinarily vigorous and courageous defense by the otherwise so mild Karl Hillebrand, this last *humane* German capable of wielding a pen. His piece appeared in the "Augsburger Zeitung"; today it can be read, in a somewhat more discreet form, in his collected writings. Here my essay was represented as an event, as a turning-point, as a first self-realization, as the best of all signs, as an actual *return* of German seriousness and German passion in matters of the spirit. Hillebrand was full of great respect for the form of the essay, for its mature taste, for its perfect tact in distinguishing between the person and the thing: he treated it with distinction as the best polemic written in German — in the act of polemics which is so dangerous, so inadvisable precisely for Germans. Unconditionally affirmative, rendered more sharply than even I had ventured to say about the going to the dogs of language in Germany (— today they play the purist and cannot construct a sentence anymore —), equally contemptuous of the "leading writers" of this nation, he ended up by expressing his admiration for my *courage* — that "supreme courage which brings charges precisely against the darlings of a nation"...The influence of this essay upon my life has been downright inestimable. Since then no one has picked a quarrel with me. People are silent, people treat me in Germany with a gloomy caution: for years I have employed an unconditional freedom of speech, for which no one today, least of all in the "Reich," has a *hand* sufficiently free. My paradise lies "under the shadow of my sword"...Basically I put into practice a maxim of Stendhal's: he advised making one's entry into society with a *duel*. And what an adversary I had chosen for myself! The foremost German freethinker!...In fact, a completely *new* kind of freethinking came about as a result: to this day nothing is more alien and unrelated to me than the entire European and American species of "*libre penseurs*." As incorrigible blockheads and buffoons of "modern ideas" I find myself in even deeper conflict with them than with any of their adversaries. They also want in their own way to "improve" mankind, in their own image; against what I am, what I *want* they would wage an implacable war, assuming they could understand it — they all still believe in the "ideal"...I am the first *immoralist* —

3

That the untimely essays designated with the names of Schopenhauer and Wagner could particularly serve in understanding or even in posing psychological questions about the two cases I should not like to avouch — with some exceptions, as is meet. Thus, for example, the elementary principle in Wagner's nature is already shown here with a deep instinct of certainty as a theatrical talent of which his means and intentions are simply the consequences. With this essay I really wanted to do something completely different from the pursuit of psychology — a problem of upbringing without equal, a new concept of *self-discipline, self-defense* to the point of hardness, a path to greatness and to world-historical tasks clamored for its first expression. By and large I took two famous and still utterly indeterminate types by the forelock, to express something, to have a few more formulas, signs, means of expression at my disposal. In the end this is also indicated with utterly uncanny sagacity (in Section 7) of the third untimely essay. Plato made use of Socrates in the same way, as a semiotic for Plato. — Now when I look back from a certain distance on that situation to which these writings bear witness, I should not wish to deny that they basically speak only to me. The essay "Wagner in Bayreuth" is a vision of my future; conversely, my innermost history, my *evolution* is inscribed in "Schopenhauer as Educator." Above all my *solemn promise!*...What I am today, where I am today — at a height where I no longer speak with words but with lightning bolts — , oh, how far I still was from this back then! — But I *sighted* land — I did not deceive myself for a moment about path, sea, peril — and success! The great tranquility in the promising, the happy looking-out on a future which shall not remain only a promise! — Here every word is experienced, profound, inward; it is not lacking in what is most painful, there are words in it that are actually bleeding. But a wind of *great* freedom blows through it all; wounds themselves make for *no* objection. — The way I understand the philosopher, as a terrible explosive before which all is in danger, the way I separate my concept of "the philosopher" miles and miles from a concept which still includes even a Kant, not to speak of academic "ruminants" and other professors of philosophy: this essay gives an invaluable lesson therein, even granted that what is basically expressed here is not "Schopenhauer as Educator," but rather its *opposite*, "Nietzsche as Educator." Considering that at that time my trade was that of a scholar and that perhaps I also *knew* my trade, the harsh piece of scholarly psychology which appears suddenly in this essay in not without significance: it expresses the *feeling of distance*, the profound certainty about what my *task* would be and what would simply be means, interlude, and side-work. It is my wisdom to have been many things and many places in order to be able to be *one thing* — in order to be able to come to *one thing*. For a time I also *had* to be a scholar. —

HUMAN, ALL-TOO-HUMAN

With Two Supplements

1

"Human, All-Too-Human" is the monument of a crisis. It calls itself a book for *free* spirits: almost every sentence in it expresses a victory — with this same book I freed myself of *that which did not belong* to my nature. Idealism does not belong to me: the title says, "Where *you* see ideal things, I see — things human, alas all-too-human!"...I know humanity *better*...In no other sense is the term "free spirit" to be understood here: a spirit *that has become free*, that has once again taken possession of itself. The tone, the sound of the voice has changed completely: one will find the book clever, cool, at times harsh and scornful. A certain spirituality of *noble* taste seems to be engaged in a perpetual struggle to keep its head above a more passionate current. In this connection there is significance in the fact that it is actually the hundredth anniversary of *Voltaire's* death which provides the excuse, as it were, for the book's publication already by the year 1878. For Voltaire is, in contrast to all who wrote after him, above all a *grandseigneur* of the spirit: which is exactly what I am too. — The name of Voltaire on an essay of mine — that was really progress — *toward myself*...If one looks more closely, one discovers a merciless spirit that knows all the hideouts where the ideal is at home — where it has its castle keeps and final security, as it were. With a torch in hand that gives off absolutely no "torch and go" light, with a penetrating brightness this *netherworld* of the ideal is brought to light. It is war, but war without powder and smoke, without warlike poses, without pathos and dislocated limbs — all this would itself still be "idealism." One error after another is put on ice, the ideal is no longer opposed — *it freezes*...Here, for example, "the genius" freezes; a little ways further "the saint" freezes; beneath a thick icicle "the hero" freezes; in conclusion "faith" freezes, so-called "conviction" freezes; "pity" also cools down considerably — almost everywhere "the thing-in-itself" freezes...

2

The beginnings of this book belong smack in the middle of the weeks of the first Bayreuth Festival; a deep alienation toward everything that surrounded me there is one of its preconditions. He who has any notions of the kind of visions which had already crossed my path at that time can guess how I felt when I woke up one day in Bayreuth. Just as if I were dreaming...Where was I then? I recognized nothing, I hardly recognized Wagner at all. In vain I leafed through the book of my recollections. Tribschen — a distant isle of the blissful: not a shadow of resemblance. The incomparable days of the cornerstone-laying, the small *affiliated* band which had celebrated them with a delicate touch not only to be wished for: not a shadow of resemblance. *What had happened?* — Wagner had been translated into German! The Wagnerian had become master over Wagner! — The *German* art! The *German* master! The *German* beer!...We others, we who know only too well to what kind of refined artists, to what cosmopolitanism of taste Wagner's art alone speaks, were beside ourselves to find Wagner bedecked with German "virtues" again. — I think I know the Wagnerian, I have "experienced" three generations of them, from the late Brendel who confused Wagner with Hegel, to the "idealists" of the Bayreuther Blaetter who confuse Wagner with themselves — I have heard all sorts of confessions of "beautiful souls" about Wagner. My kingdom for *one* intelligent word! Verily, a hair-raising crowd! Nohl, Pohl, *Kohl* (nonsense) with grace *in infinitum!* Not a single abortion is missing among them, not even the anti-Semite. — Poor Wagner! To what pass had he come? If at least he had fallen among swine! But among Germans!...Ultimately for the benefit of posterity they ought to have a genuine Bayreuther stuffed or, better yet, preserved in spirit, for spirit is what is lacking here — , with the inscription: the "spirit" upon which the "Reich" was founded looked like this...But enough! Very suddenly, in the midst of everything, I took off for a few weeks, despite the fact that a charming Parisienne tried to console me; I excused myself to Wagner solely by means of a fatalistic telegram. In a village called Klingenbrunn, hidden deep in the Boehmerwald, I carried my melancholy and my contempt for German around with me like a sickness — *and* wrote from time to time a sentence, under the general title "The Plowshare," in my notebook, nothing but *hard* psychologica which may yet be rediscovered in "Human, All-Too-Human."

3

What then resolved itself within me was not simply a breach with Wagner — I felt a total deviation of my instincts, of which any particular blunder, call it Wagner or a Basel professorship, was merely a symptom. An *impatience* with myself overcame me; I saw it was high time to get back to thinking about *myself*. All at once it became terribly clear to me how much time I had already wasted — how useless, how capricious my whole philological existence appeared compared to my task. I was ashamed of this *false* modesty...Ten years lay behind me during which the *nourishment* of my spirit was quite literally at a standstill, during which I had learned nothing useful, during which I had forgotten an absurd amount of the hodge-podge of dry-as-dust scholarship. Crawling meticulously and with bad eyesight through classical metrists — that is what I had to come to! — I was moved to pity, seeing myself quite meager, quite emaciated: *realities* were absolutely lacking in my knowledge, and the devil only knows what the "idealities" were worth! — An absolutely burning thirst laid hold of me: from then on in fact I occupied myself with nothing other than physiology, medicine, and the natural sciences — even to actual historical studies I only returned again when *the task* compelled me to do so imperiously. It was then too that I first guessed the connection between an activity chosen contrary to one's instincts, a so-called "calling" to which one is called *least of all* — and that necessity for a *deadening* of the feeling of hunger and desolation through a narcotic art — through Wagnerish art, for example. With a more careful look around I have discovered that for a great number of young men the same state of distress obtains: one unnatural action unmistakably *forces* a second. In Germany, in the "Reich," to speak unambiguously, only too many are condemned to decide too early and then to *pine away* under a burden that has become incapable of being thrown off. These types crave Wagner as an *opiate* — they forget themselves for a moment...What am I saying! — *for five or six hours!* —

4

It was then that my instinct decided inexorably against any further giving way, going along with, or taking myself for another. Any kind of life, the most unfavorable conditions, sickness, poverty — anything seemed preferable to me than that unworthy "selflessness" which I had first fallen into out of ignorance, out of *youth*, which I later hung onto out of lethargy, out of a so-called "sense of duty." — Here there came to my aid in a way I cannot sufficiently admire and at exactly the right time that *bad* inheritance on the part of my father — at bottom, a pre-determination to an early death. Sickness *slowly freed me*: it spared me any break, any violent or indecent step. I suffered no loss of goodwill at that time and even gained much in addition. At the same time my sickness gave me the right to a complete reversal of all my habits; it allowed, *it commanded* me to forget; it presented me with the *necessity* of lying-still, of idleness, of waiting and being-patient...But that means thinking!...My eyes alone put an end to all bookwormishness, in plain English, philology: I was released from "books," for years I read nothing more — the *greatest* good deed I have ever done for myself! — That most underlying self, covered over as it were, grown silent as it were under a constant *obligation to listen* to other selves (— and that is what reading means!) awakened slowly, shyly, doubtfully — but at last *it spoke again.* Never have I been so happy with myself as during the sickest and most painful periods of my life: one has to look at "Daybreak" or perhaps "The Wanderer and His Shadow" to grasp what this "return to *myself*" was: the highest sort of *recovery* itself!...The other merely followed from this. —

5

Human, All-Too-Human, this monument of a rigorous self-discipline with which I put a sudden end to all the "higher charlatanism," "idealism," "beautiful feelings," and other "femininities" that saddled me, was written down mainly in Sorrento; it was concluded and received its final form during a Basel winter under conditions far less favorable than those in Sorrento. It is really Herr *Peter Gast*, at that time a student at the University of Basel and very attached to me, who is responsible for the book. I dictated, my head bandaged and in pain, he wrote it out, he also corrected it — he was really the actual writer, while I was merely the author. When I finally had the finished product in my hand — to the profound astonishment of a seriously ill person — , I also sent two copies, among other things, to Bayreuth. Through a miraculously meaningful accident I received at the same time a handsome copy of the Parsifal text, with Wagner's dedication to me, "his dear friend Friedrich Nietzsche, from Richard Wagner, Ecclesiastical Councillor." — This crossing of the two books — it seemed to me as if I heard an ominous tone with it. Did it not sound as if two *swords* had crossed?...In any case we both felt it to be so: for we were both silent. — About this time the first Bayreuther Blaetter appeared: I grasped *for what* it was high time. — Incredible! Wagner had become pious...

6

What I thought of myself at that time (1876), with what tremendous assurance I held my task and its world-historical quality in the palm of my hand, the whole book bears witness to, especially however one very explicit passage: except that here with my instinctive cunning I also once again went around the little word "I" and this time it was not Schopenhauer or Wagner but one of my friends, the excellent Dr. Paul Rée, who was illuminated with world-historical glory — fortunately much too refined a creature to...*Others* were less refined: I have those hopeless cases among my readers, for example the typical German professor, always recognized by the fact that due to this passage he feels himself obliged to see the whole book as higher Reéalism. — In reality it contradicts five or six of my friends' propositions: one may check up on that in the preface to "The Genealogy Of Morals." — The passage reads: What then is the main proposition reached by one of the boldest and coldest thinkers, the author of the book "On The Origin Of Moral Feelings" (*lisez:* Nietzsche, the first *immoralist*), by virtue of his incisive and decisive analysis of human behavior? "The moral man stands no closer to the intelligible world than the physical man — *for* there is no intelligible world..."This proposition, hardened and sharpened under the hammer-blow of historical knowledge (*lisez: Revaluation Of All Values*) can perhaps some day in the future 1890! — serve as the ax which is laid at the root of the "metaphysical need" of mankind — whether more of a blessing or a curse to mankind, who could say? But in any case as a proposition with the weightiest consequences, fruitful and frightful at the same time and looking at the world with that Janus-face which all great knowledge has...

DAYBREAK

Thoughts About Morality as a Prejudice

With this book my campaign against *morality* begins. Not that it has the least smell of gunpowder about it — one will perceive quite other and much lovelier smells in it, assuming one's nostrils are sharp. No heavy artillery, not even any light: if the effect is negative, its means are all the less so, these means from which the effect follows like an upshot, *not* like a cannon shot. That one takes leave of the book with a timid caution toward all that has hitherto received honor and even adoration under the name of morality does not stand in opposition to the fact that no negative word is forthcoming, no attack, no malice — that it lies in the sun rather, round, happy, like a sea creature sunning itself among the rocks. In the end it was I myself who was this sea creature: almost every sentence in the book was thought up, *hatched* among that jumble of rocks near Genoa, where I was alone and still shared secrets with the sea. Even now upon casual contact with this book almost every sentence becomes for me a sharp point upon which I pull up something incomparable from the depths again: its entire skin quivers with the tender shudders of recollection. The art in which it has pre-eminence is no small one, lending a little stability to things which flit by lightly and without a sound, moments I call divine lizards — perhaps not with the cruelty of that young Greek god who simply impaled the poor little lizard, but still nevertheless with something pointed, with the pen..."There are so many dawns that have not yet broken" — this *Indian* inscription stands at the doorway to this book. Where does its author *seek* that new morn, that as yet undiscovered tender redness with which another day — ah, a whole row, a whole world of new days! — begins? In a *revaluation of all values*, in a getting free of all moral values, in being yea-saying and having confidence with all that has hitherto been forbidden, despised, damned. This *yea-saying* book sends forth its light, its love, its tenderness upon bad things one and all, it gives them back again their "soul," a good conscience, the lofty right and privilege of existence. Morality is not attacked, it is imply no longer considered...This book closes with an "Or?" — it is the only book that closes with an "Or?"...

2

My task, to prepare mankind for a moment of the highest self-contemplation, a *great noontide* when it looks back and forward, when it emerges from the domain of chance and priest and poses the question of why?, what for? For the first time as a *whole* — this task follows of necessity from the insight that mankind is *not* itself on the right path, that it is definitely *not* ruled divinely, that on the contrary, precisely among its holiest value-concepts the instinct of denial, of depravity — the *décadence*-instinct — has seductively reigned. The question of the origin of moral values is therefore for me a question of the *first rank* because it stipulates the future of mankind. The demand that we should *believe* that all is fundamentally in the best hands, that a book, The Bible, provides conclusive reassurance about divine guidance and wisdom in the destiny of mankind is, translated back into reality, the will not to let the truth be told about its pitiful opposite, namely that mankind has hitherto been in the *worst* hands, that it has been governed by those who have turned out badly, the guileful-vengeful, the so-called "saints," those world-slanderers and man-defilers. The decisive sign which reveals that the priest (including the *crypto*-priest, the philosopher) has become master, not only within a certain religious community but in general, that *décadence*-morality, the will towards the end, passes for morality *in itself*, is the unconditional value assigned to the unegoistic everywhere and the hostility assigned to the egoistic. Whoever is at odds with me on this point I consider to be *infected*...But the whole world is at odds with me...For a physiologist such an opposition in values leaves absolutely no room for doubt. When within an organism the least little organ neglects, however slightly, to carry out with utter certainty its self-preservation, its strength-compensation, its "egoism," then the whole degenerates. The phylologist demands a *cutting-out* of the degenerate part, he wants no part of it, pity for it is the furthest thing from his mind. But the priest precisely *desires* the degeneration of the whole, of mankind: therefore he *conserves* the degenerate part — at this price he rules over it...What sense is there in those lying concepts, the *helping* concepts of morality such as "soul," "spirit," "free will," "God," if not to ruin man physiologically?...When seriousness is removed from every equation concerning self-preservation, enhancement of bodily strength, *that is to say, of life*, when an ideal is construed out of anemia, "salvation of the soul" out of concept for the body, what else is it other than a *recipe* for *décadence*? — Loss of main focus, resistance to natural instincts, in a word, "selflessness" — that is what *morality* has meant thus far...With "Daybreak" I first took up the fight against the self-negating morality. —

THE GAY SCIENCE

("La Gaya Scienza")

"Daybreak" is a yea-saying book, deep, but bright and kind. The same applies once more and in the highest degree to the *gaya scienza*: in almost every sentence of this book profoundness and playfulness go softly hand in hand. A verse which expresses my thankfulness for the most wonderful month of January I have ever experienced — the whole book is a gift — , sufficiently reveals from out of what depths the "science" here has become *gay*:

> You who with a fiery spear
> Melt the ice of my soul,
> So that it roars down to the sea
> Rushing toward its highest hope:
> Ever brighter and even healthier,
> Free in most loving necessity —
> Thus it praises your wonders

Fairest January!

What is termed "highest hope" here, who could be in any doubt about it once he sees glittering at the conclusion of the fourth book the diamond beauty of the first words of Zarathustra? — Or when at the end of the third book he reads the granite sentences with which a destiny for *all time* formulates itself for the first time? — The *Songs of Prince Free-As-A-Bird*, composed for the most part in Sicily, call to mind quite expressly the Provençal concept of "gaya scienza," that unity of *singer, knight,* and *free spirit* which distinguishes that marvelous early culture of the Provençals from all ambiguous cultures; the last poem of all especially, "To The Mistral," in which morality is danced right over, is a perfect Provençalism. —

THUS SPAKE ZARATHUSTRA

A Book for All and None

1

I shall now relate the story of Zarathustra. The fundamental conception of the work, the *idea of eternal recurrence*, the highest formula of affirmation that could ever be attained — , belongs to August of the year 1881: it was jotted down hastily on a piece of paper with the inscription "6,000 feet beyond man and time." That day I was walking through the woods near Lake Surlei, beside a huge, towering, pyramidal boulder. There this idea came to me. — If I reckon back a few months from this day, I find as an omen a sudden and most profoundly decisive change in my taste, above all in music; — surely a rebirth in the art of *hearing* was one of its preconditions. In a small mountain resort not far from Vicenza, Recoaro, where I spent the spring of 1881, I discovered, together with my maestro and friend Peter

Gast, a similarly "reborn one," that the phoenix of music flew past us with lighter and brighter plumage than it had ever displayed before. If one the other hand I reckon from that day forward to the sudden delivery which took place in February 1883 under the most improbable circumstances — the last part, the same from which I have quoted a few sentences in the *preface*, was finished exactly during the hallowed hour when Richard Wagner died in Venice — thus it follows that the pregnancy lasted eighteen months. This figure of exactly eighteen months may give rise to the idea, at least among Buddhists, that I am in reality a female elephant. To this interval belonged the "*gaya scienza*," which contains a hundred signs of the nearness of something incomparable; in the end it provides even the beginning of Zarathustra itself, it provides in the next-to-last section of the fourth book the fundamental idea of Zarathustra.

— Also belonging to this interval is that *Hymn To Life* (for mixed chorus and orchestra), the score of which was published two years ago by E.W. Fritzsch in Leipzig: a perhaps not insignificant symptom of the condition of this year, when the *yea-saying* pathos par excellence, which I call the tragic pathos, dwelt within me to the highest degree. At some later day people will sing it in my memory. — The text, I expressly note since a misunderstanding about it is in circulation, is not by me: it is the amazing inspiration of a young Russian woman whom I was friends with at the time, Fräulein Lou von Salomé. Whoever can gather any meaning at all from the last words of the poem will guess why I preferred and admired it: the words have greatness. Pain does *not* count as an objection to life: "If you have no more happiness left to give me, well then! *you still have your pain...*" Perhaps my music at this point also has greatness. (Last note of the oboe: C-sharp, not C-typo.) — The following winter I stayed in that pleasant quiet bay of Rapallo not far from Genoa which cuts inland between Chiavari and the foothills of Portofino. My health was not the best; the winter cold and rainy beyond all measure; a small *albergo*, situated directly on the water, so that at night the high seas made sleep impossible, offered all in all the opposite of what would be desirable. In spite of that and almost as proof of my theory that all things decisive come about "in spite of," it was during this winter and under these unfavorable conditions that my Zarathustra came about. — In the morning I would climb in a southerly direction on the splendid road to Zoagli up in the heights, past the pines and with a view far out over the sea; in the afternoon, whenever my health permitted, I walked around the whole bay from Santa Margherita down to Portofino. This place and this countryside has come even closer to my heart through the great love which Kaiser Friedrich the Third (Emperor Frederick III) felt for it; in the fall of 1886 I chanced to be on this coast again when he paid a visit to this small forgotten world of happiness for the last time. — On these two paths the whole life of the first part of Zarathustra came to me, above all, Zarathustra himself, as a type: more correctly, *he overcame me...*

2

In order to understand this type one must first realize the physiological precondition: it is what I call *great unhealthiness*. I do not know how to explain this concept any better or *more personally* than I have already done in one of the final sections of the fifth book of the "gaya scienza." "We new, nameless, poorly understood ones" — it says there — , "we premature births of a future as yet unproved, we require for a new end a new means as well, namely, a new healthiness, a stronger, shrewder, tougher, bolder, merrier healthiness than any that has yet been. He whose soul thirsts to have experienced the whole range of hitherto existing values and desiderata and to have sailed around every coast of this ideal "Mediterranean," he who wants to know from the adventures of his own most personal experience how it feels to be a conqueror and discoverer of the ideal, as well as an artist, a saint, a lawgiver, a sage, a scholar, a pietist, a divine recluse of the old school: for that he needs one thing above all else, *great healthiness* — a healthiness one not only has but which one continually acquires and must acquire because one always relinquishes and must relinquish it...And now, after having been long underway in this way, we Argonauts of the ideal, more valiant perhaps than is prudent, and often enough shipwrecked and come to grief, but, as remarked, healthier than some would like to admit, dangerously healthy over and over again, — it would seem to us as if we have as a reward therefore a still undiscovered country before us, whose boundaries no one has yet seen, a land beyond all hitherto existing lands and cubbyholes of the ideal, a world so overly rich in things beautiful, unusual, questionable, terrible, and divine that our curiosity as well as our thirst for possession has gotten out of hand — alas, now nothing can satisfy us anymore!...With such outlooks before us and such a ravenous hunger in science and conscience, how could we still be satisfied with *present-day men*? This is bad enough, but it is inevitable that we should find it hard to maintain seriousness when looking upon his worthiest goals and hopes and perhaps not once looking upon them again...Another ideal runs ahead of us, a strange, seductive, danger-rich ideal to which we do not wish to persuade anyone because we do not easily allow anyone *the right to it*: the ideal of a spirit who naively, that is to say, unintentionally and out of an overflowing fullness and powerlessness, plays with all that was hitherto called holy, good, untouchable, godly; for whom the highest thing upon which the people rightly base their standard of value would already amount to a danger, a decay, a degradation, or, at the very least, a relaxation, a blindness, a temporary self-forgetting; the ideal of a human-superhuman well-being and well-wishing, which will often enough seem *inhuman*, for example, when placed next to all hitherto existing seriousness of this world, all hitherto existing solemnity of gesture, word, sound, look, morality, and task as their most incarnate and involuntary parody — and with which, despite all that, perhaps *the great seriousness* first commences, the actual note of interrogation is first set, the soul's destiny turns around, the clock-hand moves on, the tragedy *begins*..."

3

Has anyone at the end of the nineteenth century a distinct notion of what poets of a vigorous age meant by the word *inspiration*? If not, I will describe it. — If one had the slightest bit of superstition left in oneself, one could indeed hardly reject the idea that one is merely the incarnation, merely the mouthpiece, merely the medium of superior powers. The concept of revelation, in the sense that all of a sudden, with inexpressible certainty and subtlety, something becomes *visible*, audible, that it shakes and upsets one to the core, simply describes the facts of the case. One hears, one does not seek; one takes, one does not ask who gives; a thought flashes up like lightning, out of necessity, with no hesitancy in its form — I have never had any choice about it. A delight whose tremendous tension releases itself now and then in a torrent of tears, the pace now storming involuntarily, now becoming leisurely; a complete sense of being outside oneself with the most distinctive consciousness of an endless number of delicate shudders and shivers down to one's toes; a depth of happiness in which the most painful and dismal things do not act in contradiction but as a condition, as a positive demand, as a necessary color within such an abundance of light; an instinct for rhythmical relationships that stretches over wide spaces in terms of forms — the length, the need for a *widely-stretched* rhythm is practically the measure of the power of inspiration, a kind of compromise between push and pull...Everything takes place in the highest degree involuntarily, but as if in a storm of liberating feelings, of unconditional being, of powerfulness, of godliness...The involuntary quality of the image, of the simile is most strange; one no longer has any idea what is image, what is simile; everything offers itself as the next, the truest, the simplest expression. It actually seems, to recall a phrase of Zarathustra's, as if of themselves things came to one and offered themselves as similes (— "here all things come caressingly to your speech and flatter you: for they want to ride upon your back. Here on every simile you ride to every truth. Here the words and word-coffers of all being spring open for you; here all being wants to become word, here all being wants to learn speech from you — "). This is *my* experience of inspiration; I have no doubt that one must go back thousands of years to find someone who could say to me: "it is mine also." —

4

For a few weeks afterward I lay ill in Genoa. There followed a depressing spring in Rome, where I simply put up with life — it was not easy. Basically I was exceedingly vexed with this place which is the most unseemly on earth for the author of Zarathustra and which I had not chosen voluntarily; I tried to get away — I wanted to go to *Aquila*, the counter-concept of Rome, founded out of hostility toward Rome, as I shall one day found a place in memory of an atheist and enemy of the Church *comme il faut*, one of my closest relations, the great Hohenstaufen Emperor Frederick III. But destiny had a hand in it all; I had to go back again. In the end I resigned myself to the *piazza Barberini* after my efforts to find an *anti-Christian* quarter wore me out. I fear that in order to avoid bad smells as much as possible I once asked at the *palazzo del Quirinal* itself whether there was not a quiet room available for a philosopher. — On a *loggia* high above the said *piazza*, from which one can look far out over Rome and hear the *fontana* murmuring far below, there was composed that loveliest song that has ever been composed, the *Night Song*; at this time a melody of inexpressible melancholy surrounded me continually, whose refrain I found again in the words "dead from immortality..." In the summer, having returned to the hallowed place where the first lightning of the Zarathustra idea had flashed for me, I found the second Zarathustra. Ten days sufficed; in no case, neither in the first nor in the third and last, did I require more. The following winter, beneath the halcyon sky of Nice, which shone into my life at that time for the first time, I found the third Zarathustra — and was finished. Hardly a year for the whole thing.

Many hidden spots and heights on the countryside around Nice have been sanctified for me through unforgettable moments; that decisive section which bears the title "On Old and New Tables" was composed during the arduous ascent from the station to the marvelous Moorish rocky haunt of Eza, — my muscular dexterity was always greatest when the creative force flowed most freely. The *body* is inspired: let us leave the "soul" out of it...I might often have been seen dancing; at that time I could be on the go for seven or eight hours in the mountains without a hint of fatigue. I slept well, I laughed a great deal — , I had perfect vigor and endurance.

5

Apart from these ten-day works, the years during and above all *after* were a state of distress without equal. One pays dearly for being immortal: one dies many times in one's lifetime for it. — There is something which I call the *rancune* of greatness: everything great, a work, a deed, once it is completed, turns immediately *against* the one who did it. Precisely because he did it, he is now *weak* — he can no longer endure his deed, he can no longer look it in the eye. To have something *behind* one which one could never have willed, something in which the knot of mankind's destiny is bound up — and from now on to have it *upon* one! It is almost crushing...The *rancune* of greatness! — Another thing is the awful silence one hears around oneself. Solitude has seven skins; nothing penetrates them anymore. One comes up to men, one greets friends; a new wasteland, no glimpse of recognition greets one anymore. At best a kind of revulsion. I experienced this kind of revulsion, in very varying degrees, but from almost everyone who was close to me; it seems that nothing offends more deeply than suddenly to make one's distance felt — those *noble* natures which do not know how to live without revering are rare. — A third thing is the absurd sensitivity of the skin toward pinpricks, a kind of helplessness before all things small. This seems to me to be a product of the tremendous prodigality of defensive energies which is the precondition of every *creative* act, of every act born of one's deepest, truest, innermost being. The *small* defensive capabilities are thus, as it were, suspended; no energy flows into them anymore. — I even venture to suggest that one digests more poorly, moves less willingly, with iciness as well as mistrust being all too obvious — mistrust, which in many cases is simply an etiological blunder. In such a state I once sensed the nearness of a herd of cows even before I saw them through the return of milder, mankindlier thoughts: That has warmth in it...

6

This work stands absolutely by itself. Let us leave the poets aside: perhaps in general there has never been anything done out of a similar superfluity of strength. My concept of "Dionysian" has here become the *highest deed*; measured by it the whole rest of human activity appears poor and conditional. That a Goethe, a Shakespeare would be unable to breathe for even a moment, taking into account this tremendous passion and elevation; that Dante, compared to Zarathustra, is merely a believer and not one who first *creates* the truth, a *world-governing* spirit, a destiny — , that the poets of the Veda are not even worthy to unloose the latchet of a Zarathustra's shoes, all that is of the least importance and gives no idea of the distance, of the *azure* solitude in which this work dwells. Zarathustra has an eternal right to say: "I form circles around me and holy boundaries; ever fewer climb with me on ever higher mountains — I build a mountain range out of ever holier mountains." Add up the spirit and goodness of all greats souls into one: all together they would not be capable of producing one of Zarathustra's speeches. The ladder is tremendous upon which he climbs up and down; he has seen further, willed further, *been capable of* further than any other than man. He contradicts with every word, this most yea-saying of all beings; in him all things contradictory are brought together in a new unity. The highest and the lowest powers of human nature, the sweetest, most frivolous, most frightful things stream forth from *one* fountain with undying certainty. Until then one did not know what was height, what was depth; one knew even less what truth is. There is not one moment in this revelation of the truth which would have been anticipated at all, divined by *one* of the greatest. There is no wisdom, no exploration of the soul, no art speech before Zarathustra: the nearest, the most ordinary here speaks the most unheard of things. Sentences trembling with passion; rhetoric become music; lightning-bolts hurled ahead toward hitherto undivined futures. The mightiest strength for comparison that has yet existed is paltry and child's play compared with this return of language to the nature of imagery. — And how Zarathustra descends and says the kindliest things to everyone! How he treats even his adversaries, the priests, with gentle hands, and suffers from them with them! — Here at every moment man is surpassed, here the concept of "Superman" has become the greatest reality, — everything that has hitherto been called great in man lies at an infinite distance *beneath* him. The halcyon, the light feet, the omnipresence of malice and exuberance and whatever else is typical of the Zarathustra type has never been dreamed of as essential to greatness. It is precisely in this compass of space, in this openness to opposites that Zarathustra feels himself to be the *highest species of all beings*; and when you hear how he defines this, you will give up trying to find his equal.

> — the soul which has the longest ladder and can go down the deepest,
>
> the most extensive soul, which can run and ramble and roam the furthest within itself,
>
> the most essential soul, which hurls itself with pleasure into chance,
>
> the being soul which insists upon becoming, the having soul which *insists upon* willing and longing — ,
>
> the self-fleeing soul, which catches up with itself in the widest sphere,
>
> the wisest soul, which folly sweet-talks the most,
>
> the most self-loving soul, in which all things have their current and counter-current and ebb and flow — —

But this is the concept of Dionysus himself. — Another consideration leads to the same thing. The psychological problem in the Zarathustra type is how he, who to an unheard of degree says No, *does* No to everything to which people have hitherto said Yes, can nevertheless be the opposite of a nay-saying spirit; how he, a spirit bearing the heaviest of destinies, a fatality of a task, can nevertheless be the lightest and most opposite to that — Zarathustra is a dancer — : how he, who has the harshest, most frightful insight into reality, who has thought the "most abysmal thoughts," nevertheless finds in that no objection to existence — rather one more reason *to be himself* the eternal Yes to all things, "the enormous, unbounded Yea-and Amen-saying"..."Into all abysses I still carry my blessed Yea-saying"...*But this is the concept of Dionysus once more.*

7

— What language will such a spirit speak when he speaks to himself alone? The language of the *dithyramb*. I am the inventor of the dithyramb. Hear how Zarathustra speaks to himself *before sunrise*: such emerald happiness, such godly tenderness had not yet found a voice before I came along. Even the deepest melancholy of such a Dionysus still becomes a dithyramb; I pick, as testimony, the *Night Song* — the immortal lament of one condemned not to love because of his superabundant light and might, because of his *sun-like* nature.

> It is night: now all gushing fountains speak louder. And my soul too is a gushing fountain.
> It is night: only now do all lovers' songs awake. And my soul too is the song of a lover.
> Something unappeased, unappeasable is within me; it wants to be heard. A craving for love is within me which itself speaks the language of love.
> Light am I: ah to be night! But this is my loneliness, to be girded with light.
> Ah, to be dark and nightly! How I would suck on the breasts of the light!
> And even you would I bless, you twinkling little stars and glow

worm up above! — and be blessed by your gifts of light.

But I live in my own light, I take back into me the flames that break out of me.

I know not the happiness of the receiver; and often have I dreamed that stealing must be even more blessed than receiving.

This is my poverty, that my hand never rests from giving; this is my envy, that I see waiting eyes and the illuminated nights of longing.

O, the unhappiness of all givers! O, eclipse of my sun! O, craving to crave! O, ravenous appetite in satiety!

They take from me: but do I ever touch their souls? There is a cleft between giving and receiving; and the smallest cleft is the last to be spanned.

A hunger grows out of my beauty: I would like to hurt those for whom I shine, I would like to rob those whose gifts were mine — thus I hunger after malice.

Drawing back the hand when a hand is already stretched out for it; hesitating like the waterfall, which hesitates even in its sudden plunge — thus I hunger after malice.

Such vengeance my abundance thinks up, such maliciousness wells up out of my loneliness.

My happiness in giving died in giving, my virtue grew weary of itself by virtue of its excess!

The danger for him who always gives is that he will lose his shame; the hand and heart of him who always dispenses has calluses from nothing but dispensing.

My eye no longer overflows over the shame of the supplicant; my hand has grown too hard for the trembling of filled hands.

Where have the tears in my eyes gone, and the bloom in my heart? O, the loneliness of all givers! O, the quietness of all light-givers!

Many suns revolve in empty space: to all that is dark they speak with their light — to me they are silent.

O, this is the light's enmity toward the giver of light: mercilessly it travels its course.

Unjust toward the giver of light in its heart of hearts, cold toward other suns — thus every sun travels.

Like a storm the suns fly along their course, that is their travel. Their inexplicable will they follow, that is their coldness.

O, it is only you, you dark ones, you nightly ones, who create your warmth from the giver of light! O, only you drink milk and comfort from the udders of the light!

Alas, ice is all around me, my hand burns itself on the icy! Alas, a thirst is in me that yearns for your thirst!

It is night: alas that I must be light! And have a thirst for the nightly! And loneliness!

It is night: now my longing bursts out of me like a fountain

— for speech I long.

It is night: now all gushing fountains speak louder. And my soul too is a gushing fountain.

It is night: only now do all lovers' songs awake. And my soul too is the song of a lover. —

8

The like of this has never been written, never been felt, never been *suffered*: thus suffers a god, a Dionysus. The reply to such a dithyramb on a sun's isolation in the light would be *Ariadne*...Who besides me knows what Ariadne is!...For all such riddles no one has hitherto had the solution; I even doubt whether anyone ever saw a riddle here. — One time Zarathustra strictly determines his task — it is mine also — the *meaning* of which one cannot be mistaken: he is yea-saying to the point of vindication, to the point of redemption even of all things past.

I walk among men as among the fragments of the future: that future into which I look.

And this is my every word and deed, to compose and collect into one what is fragment and riddle and terrible accident.

And how could I stand being a man if man were not also the composer, riddle-reader, and redeemer of chance?

To redeem what is past and remold every "It was" into "I willed it so!" — only that would I call redemption.

In another passage he defines as strictly as possible what "man" alone can be for him — *not* an object of love or even of pity — over the *great loathing* of man Zarathustra has also become master: to him man is something unformed, mere substance, an ugly stone in need of a sculptor.

No more *willing* and no more *valuing* and no more creating! O, may that great weariness always remain far from me!

In knowing as well as I feel only my will's pleasure in begetting and becoming; and if there is innocence in my knowledge, then it is because the *will to beget* is in it.

Away from God and gods this will has enticed me: what would there be to create then if gods — were there?

But always it drives me back again to men, my fervent creative will;

thus the hammer is driven to the stone.

Alas, you men, an image sleeps in the stone for me, the image of my image! Alas, that it must sleep in the hardest, homeliest stone!

Now my hammer rages cruelly against its prison. From the stone pieces scatter: what does that matter to me?

I want to complete it; for a shadow came to me — the stillest and lightest of all things came to me!

The beauty of the Superman came to me as a shadow: of what regard to me now are — the gods!...

I call special attention to one last viewpoint: the italicized line provides the occasion for it. The hardness of the hammer, the *joy even in destruction*, are in a decisive way part of the preliminary conditions for a *Dionysian* task. The imperative: "become hard!," the deepest certainty *that all creators are hard* is the true mark of distinction of a Dionysian nature. —

BEYOND GOOD AND EVIL

Prelude to a Philosophy of the Future

1

The task for the immediately following years was marked out as clearly as possible. After the yea-saying part of my task was resolved, it now came time for the nay saying, *nay-doing* half: the revaluation of all hitherto existing values themselves, the great war — the evocation of a Judgment Day. Included here is the slow search for kindred spirits, for those who out of strength, could lend a hand in the task of *destruction*. — From then on all of my writings become fishing hooks: perhaps I understand as well as anyone how to fish?...If nothing got caught, it is not my fault. *There were no fish...*

2

This book (1886) is in all essentials a *critique of modernity*, modern science, modern art, even modern politics, along with indications of an opposite type that is anything but modern, a noble, yea-saying type. In the latter sense the book is a *school for gentlemen*, the concept taken more spiritually and *more radically* than it has ever been taken before. Even to endure it one must have heart, one must never have learned fear...All the things of which our era is proud are felt to be contrary to this type, as bad manners almost, our famous "objectivity" for instance, our "sympathy with all that suffers," our "historical sense" with its submissiveness before foreign tastes, with its lying on its belly before *petit faits*, its "scientificality." — If one considers that it comes after Zarathustra, then one can also perhaps divine the dietetic *régime* to which it owes its origin. The eye, spoiled by a tremendous compulsion *to see far* — Zarathustra is even more far-seeing than the czar — , is here forced to sharply grasp what is nearest, the time at hand, what is *around us*. In all the bits and pieces, and above all in the form, one will find the same *voluntary* instincts which made a Zarathustra possible. The refinement in form, in design, in the art of *keeping silent* is in the foreground; psychology is handled with an admitted hardness and cruelty — the book dispenses with every good-natured word...All this is refreshing: — Who could ultimately guess *what* kind of refreshment is necessitated by such an expenditure of goodness as is found in Zarathustra?...Theologically speaking — listen, for I rarely speak as a theologian — it was God himself who at the end of his day's work lay down as a serpent under the tree of knowledge: thus he rested from being God...He had made everything too beautiful...The devil is merely God's idleness on that seventh day...

GENEALOGY OF MORALS

A Polemic

The three essays of which this genealogy consists are with regard to expression, purpose, and the art of surprise perhaps the uncanniest that have ever been written. Dionysus is, as you know, also the god of darkness. — Each time a beginning that is *meant* to mislead, cool, scientific, ironic, purposely foreground, purposely keeping one in suspense. Gradually more unrest; scattered summer lightning; very unpleasant truths making themselves heard from afar with dull rumbling sounds — until finally a *tempo feroce* is attained in which everything rushes forward with tremendous tension. In conclusion each time amid utterly horrible detonations a *new* truth visible between thick clouds. — The truth of the *first* essay is the psychology of Christianity: the birth of Christianity out of the spirit of resentment, *not*, as is generally believed, out of the "spirit" — a counter-movement essentially, the great rebellion against the dominion of *noble* values. The *second* essay presents the psychology of *conscience*: it is *not*, as is generally believed, "the voice of God in man" — it is the instinct of cruelty turned back upon itself after it can no longer discharge itself outside. Cruelty as one of the oldest and most unrationalizable cultural substrata brought here to light for the first time. The *third* essay provides the answer to the question where the tremendous *power* of the ascetic ideal, the priestly ideal, comes from, although it is the *pernicious* ideal *par excellence*, a will to the end, an ideal of *décadence*. Answer: *not* because God is busy at work behind the priests, as is generally believed, but *faute de mieux* — because it has been the only ideal thus far, because it has had no rivals. "For man would rather will even nothing than *not* will at all"...What was lacking above all was a *counter-ideal* — *until the coming of Zarathustra.* — I have been understood. Three decisive preliminary studies by a psychologist for a revaluation of all values. — This book contains the first psychology of the priest.

How One Philosophizes with a Hammer

1

This work of not quite 150 pages, cheerful and fateful in tone, a demon that laughs — , the work of so few days that I hesitate to mention the number is among books in general the exception: there is nothing more rich in substance, more independent, more subversive — more wicked. If you would like to get a brief idea of how before me everything was standing on its head, then start with this work. That which is called *idols* on the title page is quite simply that which has hitherto been termed truth. *Twilight of the Idols* — in plain English: the old truth is on its way out...

2

There is no reality, no "ideality" which is not touched in this writing (— what a careful euphemism!...). Not only the *eternal* idols, also the most recent, hence the most senile. "Modern ideas," for example. A great big wind blows among the trees and everywhere fruits fall down — truths. There is the lavishness of an all-too-rich autumn in it: one trips over truths, one even tramples some to death — there are too many of them...But the ones you get your hands on are no longer questionable, they are something decisive. I alone possess the yardstick for "truths" in my hand, I alone *am able to* decide. Just as if a *second consciousness* had arisen in me, just as if "the will" had kindled in me a light for itself over the false track upon which it had previously run downwards...The false track — they called that the way to "truth"...All "dark aspiration" is at an end, it is precisely: the "good man" who has been least aware of the right way...And in all seriousness, before me no one knew the right way, the way *upwards*: only beginning with me are there once again hopes, tasks, perceivable cultural paths — *I am the bringer of these glad tidings*...Precisely because of that I am also a destiny. — —

3

Immediately after completing the aforementioned work and without losing even a day, I took on the immense task of the *Revaluation* with a sovereign feeling of pride beyond compare, certain every moment of my immortality and engraving sign after sign on brass tablets with the certainty of a destiny. The foreword came about on September 3rd, 1888: the morning after writing this down, when I stepped outside, I found before me the finest day the Ober-Engadin had ever shown me — clear, glowing with colors, including all the contrasts, all the middle states between ice and south. — Only on September 20th did I leave Sils-Maria, detained there by floods, in the end the sole guest by far of this wonderful place upon which my gratitude wishes to bestow the gift of an immortal name. After an incident-filled journey, with even life-threatening danger at flooded Como, which I only reached in the dead of night, I arrived on the afternoon of the 21st in Turin, my *proven* place, my residence from now on. I took again the same lodgings I had occupied in the spring, *via Carlo Alberto* 6, III, opposite the mighty *palazzo Carignano*, in which *Vittorio Emanuele* was born, with a view of the *piazza Carlo Alberto* and of the hill-country beyond. Without hesitation and without allowing myself a moment's rest, I went back to work: only the last quarter of the book was still waiting to be done. On the 30th of September great victory; seventh day; idleness of a god along the banks of the Po. On the same day I also wrote the *foreword* to "Twilight Of The Idols," the correction of whose proofs had been my recreation in September. — I have never experienced such an autumn, nor deemed anything of the sort possible on earth — a Claude Lorrain imagined into infinity, with every day composed of the same boundless perfection. —

THE CASE OF WAGNER

A Musician's Problem

1

In order to be fair to this work one must suffer from the fate of music as from an open wound. — *From what* do I suffer when I suffer from the fate of music? From this, that music has been robbed of its world-transfiguring, yea-saying character, that it is *décadence*-music, and no longer the flute of Dionysus...Supposing, however, that a person thus feels the cause of music as his *own* cause, as his own passion play, then he will find this work full of deference and mild beyond measure. To be cheerful under such circumstances and jeer at oneself good-naturedly — *ridendo dicere severum*, when the *verum dicere* would justify any degree of hardness — is humanity itself. Who really doubts that I, old artillerist that I am, have the capacity to bring up my heavy guns against Wagner? — I held back on everything decisive in this matter — I have loved Wagner. — Ultimately, an attack upon a more artful "unknown" not easily divined by anyone else is part and parcel of my task — oh, I still have completely different "unknowns" to unmask other than a Cagliostro of music — even more, of course, an attack upon the German nation which is growing ever lazier and more instinct-impoverished in spiritual things, growing ever more honorable, which continues to subsist with an enviable appetite on opposites, gulping down "faith" as well as things of a scientific nature, "Christian love" as well as anti-Semitism, the will to power (to the "Reich") as well as *évangile des humbles* without any indigestion...This lack of faction between opposites! This stomachic neutrality and "selflessness"! This just sense of the German *palate* which accords equal rights to all — which finds everything tasty...Without any doubt whatsoever, the Germans are idealists...

2

But here nothing shall stop me from being rude and telling the Germans a few hard truths: *who would do it otherwise?* — I speak of their indecency . Not simply that the German historians have altogether lost the *big picture* when it comes to the course, to the values of culture, that they are all of them buffoons of politics (or of the Church —): this big picture itself has been *proscribed* by them. One must be "German" first of all, one must have "race," then one can decide all values and disvalues *in historicis* — one lays them down..."German" is also an argument, "Deutschland, Deutschland ueber alles" a principle, the Teutons a "moral world-order" in history; in relation to the *imperium Romanum* they are the representatives of freedom, in relation to the eighteenth century the restorers of morality, of the "categorical imperative"...There is an Imperial German historiography, there is, I fear, even an anti-Semitic one, — there is a court historiography and Herr von Treitschke is not ashamed...Recently an idiotic judgment *in historic*, a proposition of the happily late Swabian aesthetician Vischer, made the round of the German newspaper as a "truth to which every German *had to say yes*: "The Renaissance *and* the Reformation, only both of them together make up a whole — the aesthetic rebirth *and* the moral rebirth." — Propositions such as these exhaust my patience and I sense the desire, I even feel it a duty, to tell the Germans for once *what* they already have on their conscience. *All the great culture-crimes of the last four centuries they have on their conscience!*...And always for the same reason, out of their innermost *cowardice* before reality, which is also cowardice before the truth; out of the untruthfulness which has become instinct for them, out of "idealism"...The Germans have robbed Europe of the harvest of the last *great* era, the Renaissance era, at a moment when a higher order of values, when the noble, life-affirming, future-assuring values had achieved victory at the seat of their opposite, the *values of decline — and down into the very instincts of those sitting there*! Luther, that disaster of a monk, restored the Church and, what was a thousand times worse, Christianity, at the moment *when it lay defeated*...Christianity, that *denial of the will to life* become religion!...Luther, an impossible monk who, for reasons of "impossibility," attacked the Church and — consequently! Restored it...The Catholics would have good reason to celebrate Luther feasts, to write Luther plays...Luther — and the "moral rebirth!" To hell with all psychology! — Without a doubt the Germans are idealists. — Two times, just when with a tremendous valor and self-overcoming an upright, unequivocal, utterly scientific way of thinking had been attained, the Germans knew how to find a secret path back to the old "ideal," reconciliations between truth and the "ideal," at the bottom, formulae for a right to reject science, for a right to *falsehood*. Leibniz and Kant — those two greatest impediments to the intellectual integrity to Europe! — Finally, when there appeared on the bridge spanning two centuries of *décadence* a *force majeure* of genius and will strong enough to create a unity out of Europe, a political and *economic* unity designed to rule the world, the Germans, with their "Wars of Liberation," robbed Europe of the meaning, of the wonderful meaning of Napoleon's existence — hence they have everything that came after, everything that exists here today on their conscience, this *most cultural-inimical* sickness and unreasonableness that there is, nationalism, this *névrose nationale* with which Europe is sick, this perpetuation of European petty-statesmanship, of *petty* politics: they have robbed Europe itself of its meaning, of its *reason* — they have led it into a blind alley. — Does anyone besides me know a way out of this blind alley?...A task great enough to *bind* the nations once again?...

3

— And in the end, why should I not give voice to my suspicion? In my case as well as the Germans will try to give birth out of a tremendous destiny to a mouse. They have compromised themselves with me up till now, I doubt they will do any better in the future. Ah, how I wish here I were a *false* prophet!...My natural readers and listeners even now are Russians, Scandinavians, and French — will it be so evermore? — The Germans are written down in the history of knowledge with nothing but double-dealing names, they have produced "unconscious" counterfeiters (— this term applies to Fichte, Schelling, Schopenhauer, Hegel, and Schleiermacher, as well as Kant and Leibniz; they are all merely Schleiermacher (veil-makers) —): they should never have the honor that the first *upright* spirit in the history of the spirit should have, the spirit in whom truth sits in judgment over the counterfeiting of four millennia, with which the German spirit is reckoned as one. "German spirit" is *my* bad air: I breathe poorly in the neighborhood of this impurity become instinct *in psychologicis*, which in every word and expression betrays a German. They have never gone through a seventeenth century hard self-examination like the French — a La Rochefoucauld, a Descartes are a hundred times superior to the foremost Germans in integrity — , until today they have had no psychologists. But psychology is practically the yardstick for the *purity* or the *impurity* of a race...And if one is not yet cleansed, how can one have *depth*? With Germans, much as with women, one cannot fathom their depth: *they have none*: that is all. But in that case they are not even shallow. — What in Germany is called "deep" is precisely this instinctive unseemliness towards oneself which I just spoke of: they *will* not be clear about themselves. Might I not propose the word "German" as an international coinage for this psychological depravity? — At this moment for example the German Kaiser calls it his "Christian duty" to free the slaves in Africa: among us *other* Europeans that would simply be called "German"...Have the Germans ever produced a book that had any depth? The very idea of depth in a book is lost on them. I have met scholars who considered Kant deep; at the Prussian court, I fear, they consider Herr von

Treitschke deep. And when on occasion I came to praise Stendhal as a deep psychologist, I have encountered German professors who asked me to spell his name...

4

— And why should I not proceed to the end. I like to make a clean sweep. It is even part of my ambition to be considered a despiser of Germans *par excellence*. Already at the age of twenty-six I expressed my mistrust of the German character (Third Untimely Essay [Section 6]) — the Germans are impossible for me. Whenever I imagine a kind of man that runs counter to all my instincts, it always turns out to be a German. The first way in which I "test the reins" with a man is whether he has an intrinsic sense of distance, whether he sees rank, order, and distance everywhere among men, whether he *makes distinctions*: with this one is a *gentilhomme*; in every other case one irrevocably falls under the open-hearted, alas! so very good-natured concept of the *canaille*. But the Germans are *canaille*— alas! They are so good-natured...One lowers oneself by associating with Germans: the German *equalizes*...Take away my association with a few artists, above all with Richard Wagner, and I have not passed one good hour with Germans...Suppose that the profoundest spirit of all millennia appeared among the Germans, some goose-savior of the capitol would imagine that his very unbeautiful soul should receive at least the same consideration...I cannot endure this race with whom one is always in bad company, which has no fingers for *nuances* — woe is me! I am a nuance — , which has no *esprit* in its feet and cannot even walk...In the end the Germans have no feet at all, they only have legs...The Germans have no idea how vulgar they are; but that is the highest degree of vulgarity — they are not even *ashamed* of being merely Germans... They have something to say about everything, they even regard themselves as decisive, I am afraid they have even decided about me...My whole life is the proof *de rigueur* of these propositions. In vain I seek in that life for a sign of tact, *of délicatesse* toward me. From the Jews yes, never yet from Germans. My nature ordains it that I be gentle and benevolent towards everyone — I have a *right* not to make distinctions — : this does not prevent me from having my eyes open. I except no one, least of all my friends, — I hope in the end this has not diminished my humanity towards them! There are five or six things which have always been a point of honor with me. — Nevertheless it remains true that almost every letter that has reached me for years now strikes me as a piece of cynicism: there is more cynicism in goodwill toward me than in any hatred...I tell each one of my friends to his face that he has never found it worth the trouble to *study* any of my writings: I can guess from the smallest signs that they do not even know what is in them. And as for my Zarathustra, who among my friends would have seen more in it than an impermissible though fortunately utterly harmless piece of arrogance?...Ten years: and no one in Germany has felt duty-bound to defend my name against the absurd silence under which it lies buried: it was a foreigner, a Dane, who first had enough fineness of instinct *and* fortitude to do this, who was enraged at my so-called friends...At which German university today would lectures on my philosophy be possible such as were held last spring in Copenhagen by Dr. Georg Brandes, thereby proving himself once more a philosopher? — I myself have never suffered from all this; what is *necessary* does not offend me; *amor fati* describes my innermost nature. This does not, however, rule out my love of irony, even world historical irony. And so, approximately two years before the shattering thunderclap of the *Revaluation* which will set the world into convulsions, I have sent the "Case Of Wagner" into the world: the Germans were obliged to eternally mistake me once more and *immortalize* themselves! There is just enough time for it yet! — Has it been achieved? Delightfully, my dear Teutons! My compliments to you...

WHY I AM A DESTINY

1

I know my lot. One day my name will be connected with the recollection of something enormous — with a crisis like never before on earth, with the deepest clash of conscience, with a decision solely invoked against all that had until then been believed, demanded, hallowed. I am not a man, I am dynamite. — And with all that there is nothing in me to suggest the founder of a religion — religions are rabble-affairs, I find it necessary to wash my hands after contact with religious people...I *desire* no "believers," I think I am too malicious even to believe in myself, I never speak to the masses...I have a terrible fear that one day I will be pronounced *holy*: one can guess why I bring out this book *beforehand*, it should prevent them from doing mischief with me...I have no wish to be a saint, I would rather be a buffoon...Perhaps I am a buffoon...And nevertheless or rather *not* nevertheless — for thus far there has been nothing more mendacious than saints — the truth speaks out of me. — But my truth is *frightful*: for thus far the lie has been called truth. — *Revaluation of all Values*: that is my formula for an act of the highest examination on the part of mankind, which has become flesh and genius in me. My lot decrees that I must be the first *decent* man, to know that I stand opposed to the falseness of millennia...I was the first to *discover* the truth in that I was the first to sense the lie as lie — to *smell* it...My genius lies in my nostrils...I contradict as has never been contradicted before and am nevertheless the opposite of a nay-saying spirit. I am a *bringer of glad tidings* like there never was before, I am acquainted with tasks of such loftiness that the concept of them has been lacking; only starting with me are there hopes again. With all that I am necessarily also the man of disaster. For when truth enters into battle with the lies of millennia, we shall have convulsions, a spasm of earthquakes, a displacing of mountain and valley the like of which has never been dreamed. The concept of politics will then be completely taken up with spiritual warfare, all the power structures of the old society will be blown sky high — they all rest on lies: there will be wars like never before on earth. Only starting with me is there *grand politics* on earth. —

2

Do you want a formula for such a destiny *become man*? It is contained in my Zarathustra.

> — and he who would be a creator in good and evil, he must first be a destroyer and shatter values.

> Thus the highest evil belongs to the highest good: that, however is the creative.

I am by far the most terrible man yet; this does not rule out the fact that I shall be the most beneficial. I know the joy in *destruction* to a degree commensurate with my *power* of destruction, — in both I obey my Dionysian nature, which does not know how to separate the no-doing from the yea-saying. I am the first *immoralist*: in this I am the *destroyer par excellence*.

3

I have not been asked, as I should have been asked, precisely what he name of *Zarathustra* means in my mouth, in the mouth of the first immoralist: for what constitutes the tremendous historical uniqueness of that Persian is precisely the opposite of this. Zarathustra was the first to see in the struggle of good and evil the true wheel in the working of things — the translation of morality into the metaphysical, as force, first cause, end-in-itself, is *his* work. But this question is basically already the answer. Zarathustra *created* this most fateful of errors, morality: consequently he must also be the first to recognize it as such. Not only that here he has longer and greater experience than any other thinker — all of history is indeed the experimental refutation of the proposition of a so-called "moral world-order" — : the more important thing is that Zarathustra is more truthful than any other thinker. His doctrine, and his alone, defines truthfulness as the highest virtue — that is to say, the opposite of the *cowardice* of the "idealist" who takes flight in the face of reality; Zarathustra has more bravery in his body than all other thinkers put together. To speak truth and *shoot well with bow and arrow*, that is the Persian virtue. — Am I understood?...The self-overcoming of morality through truthfulness, the self-overcoming of the moralist into his opposite — *into me* — that is precisely what the name of *Zarathustra* means in my mouth.

4

Basically there are two negations implied in my term immoralist. First I deny the type of man hitherto considered the highest, the *good* man, the *benevolent* man, *the beneficent* man; secondly I deny a kind of morality which has gained currency and mastery as morality-in-itself — *décadence*-morality, in cruder terms, Christian morality. It would be acceptable to view the second contradiction as the more decisive, since the over-valuation of goodness I already regard as a consequence of *décadence*, as a symptom of weakness, as incompatible with an ascending and yea-saying life: negating *and destroying* are conditions of yea-saying. For now I will stay with the psychology of the good man. In order to assess what a type of man is worth, one must calculate the price paid for his preservation — one must be acquainted with the conditions of his existence. The existence of the good is conditioned by *falsehood*: expressed differently, the not *wanting* at any price to see how reality is really constituted, namely not in such a way as to demand benevolent instincts from it at all times, even less so as to be pleased at the interference of short-sighted, good-natured hands. To consider all *distress-states* as an objection, as something that must be *abolished*, is the *niaiserie par excellence*, reckoned by and large, a true disaster in its consequences, a fatal stupidity — , almost as stupid as the will to abolish bad weather would be — out of pity for the poor perhaps...In the great economy of the whole, the frightful aspects of reality (in affects, in desires, in the will to power) are to an incalculable degree more necessary than that form of petty happiness, the so-called "goodness"; it is sheer indulgence to grant the latter any place at all, since it is conditioned by an instinct of mendacity. I shall have the grand opportunity of showing for the whole of history the consequences, ghastly beyond all measure, of *optimism*, that misshapen offspring of the *homines optimi*. Zarathustra, the first to grasp that the optimist is just as *décadent* as the pessimist and perhaps more pernicious, says: *good men never tell the truth. False shores and false assurances the good have taught you; you have been born and harbored in the falsehoods of the good. Everything has been thoroughly hooked and crooked by the good.* Fortunately the world is not built on those instincts precisely wherein the merely good-natured herd animal would find his narrow happiness; to demand that everyone should be a "good man," a herd animal, a blue-eyed, benevolent "beautiful soul" — or, as Mr. Herbert Spencer would have it, altruistic, which would mean robbing existence of its *great* character, would mean castrating mankind and bringing it down to a pathetic Chinadom. — *And this is what they have tried to do!...Precisely this has been called morality!...*In this sense Zarathustra first calls the good " the last men," then later "the beginning of the end"; above all, he finds them the *most harmful kind of man*, because they secure their existence at the expense of *truth* just as they do at the expense of the *future*.

The good — they cannot *create*, they are always the beginning of the end. —

— they crucify the one who writes *new* values on new tables, they sacrifice the future *to themselves*, they crucify all man's future!

The good — they have always been the beginning of the end...

And whatever harm the world-slanderers may do, *the harm the good do is the most harmful harm.*

5

Zarathustra, the first psychologist of the good, is — consequently — a friend of the wicked. When a *décadence* type of man has risen to the rank of being the highest type, this can only take place at the expense of its opposite type, the type of man who is strong and certain of life. When the herd animal sparkles in the brilliance of the purest virtue, then the exceptional man must be downgraded to evil. When mendacity at any price appropriates the word "truth" for its perspective, than the really truthful must be found again under the worst names. Zarathustra leaves no room for doubt here: he says it was precisely his knowledge of the good, of the " "best" which caused his horror of man in general; out of *this* aversion he grew wings "to soar off into distant futures" — he does not hide the fact that *his* type of man, a relatively superhuman type, is superhuman precisely in relation to the good, that the *good* and the just would call his Superhuman *devil*...

> You highest of men my eye has met, this is what I doubt in you and secretly laugh about: I suspect that you would call my Superman — devil!

> Such a stranger you are in your souls to what is great, that to you the Superman would be *frightful* in his goodness...

It is at this point and nowhere else that one must a start in order to grasp what Zarathustra wants: the type of man that he depicts, depicts reality *as it is*: this type is strong enough for that — , he is not estranged from it, not carried away by it; he is *reality itself,* he has in himself as well all its terrible and questionable things; *only in this way can man have greatness...*

6

— But there is also another sense in which I have chosen the word *immoralist* as a mark of distinction, as a badge of honor for myself; I am proud to possess this word which makes me stand out from the rest of mankind. No one yet has felt *Christian* morality as being *beneath* him: that requires a height, a farsightedness, a hitherto quite unheard-of psychological depth and precipitousness. Christian morality has hitherto been the Circe of all thinkers — they stand in her service. — Who before me has climbed down into the caverns from which the poisonous breath of this kind of ideal-*world-calamity* — wells up? Who has ever dared to suspect *that* they are caverns? Who before me among philosophers in general has been a *psychologist* and not on the contrary its opposite, a "higher swindler," an "idealist"? Before me there was absolutely no psychology. — To be the first here can be a curse, it is in any case a destiny: *for as the first one also despises...*The *disgust* with man is my danger...

7

Have I made myself understood? — What defines me, what sets me apart from the whole rest of mankind is that I have *unmasked* Christian morality. That is why I needed a word that comprised a sense of challenge to everyone. Not to have opened its eyes sooner here strikes me as the greatest unseemliness that mankind has on its conscience, as self-deceit become instinct, as the fundamental will *not* to see every happening, every causality, every reality as counterfeiting in *psychologicis* to the point of being a crime. Blindness in the presence of Christianity is the *crime par excellence* — the crime *against life...*The millennia, the peoples, the first as well as the last, the philosophers and the old ladies — except for five or six moments in history, me being the seventh — in this respect they all deserve each other. The Christian has hitherto been *the* "moral being," a curiosity without equal — and, *as* a "moral being" more absurd, vain, mendacious, frivolous, *injurious to himself* than even the greatest despiser of mankind could ever have dreamed. Christian morality — the most malevolent form of the will to the lie, the real Circe of mankind: that which has ruined it. It is *not* the error as error whose aspect fills me with terror, *not* the thousand-year-long lack of "good will" , of breeding, of bearing, of bravery in spiritual things which betrays itself in this victory — it is the lack of nature, it is the utterly dreadful fact that *anti-nature* itself took home the highest honors and has remained hanging over mankind as law, as categorical imperative!...To blunder in this way, *not* as an individual, not as a people, but as mankind in general!...That contempt has been taught for the primary instincts in life, that a "soul," a "spirit" has been *falsely invented* in order to destroy the body; that people have been taught to feel something unclean in the prerequisite of life, in sexuality; that the evil principle has been sought in the deepest necessity for flourishing, in *strict* egoism (— the very word is slanderous! —); that, conversely, in the typical signs of decline and instinct-contradiction, in being "selfless," in the loss of center of gravity, in "depersonalization" and "neighbor-love" (— neighbor *mania!*) one sees the *higher* value, what am I saying, the *value-in-itself!* ...What! Could mankind itself be in a state of *décadence?* Has it always been? What is certain is that it has been *taught* only *décadence* values as the highest values. The morality of self-negation is the morality of decline *par* excellence, the fact "I am going to ruin" translated into the imperative: "You *shall* all go to ruin" — and *not only* in the imperative!...This only morality that has been taught thus far, the morality of self-negation, reveals a will to the end, it *negates* life at its very foundation. — The possibility still remains that it is not mankind which is degenerating but only that parasitical species of man, the *priest,* who armed with morality has lied his way into a value-determining position — who has divined in Christian morality his means to *power*...And indeed, this is *my* insight: the teachers, the leaders of mankind, the theologians one and all, have also been *décadents* one and all: *hence* the revaluation of all values into hostility toward life, hence morality...*Definition of morality:* morality — the idiosyncrasy of *décadents,* with the hidden agenda of *revenging themselves upon life* — *and* succeeding. I set great store on this definition. —

8

— Have I made myself understood? — I have not said one word here which I did not already say five years ago through the mouth of Zarathustra. — The *unmasking* of Christian morality is an event unequaled, an actual catastrophe. He who throws light upon it is a *force majeure*, a destiny — he breaks in two the history of mankind. One lives *before* him, one lives *after* him...The lightning bolt of truth strikes precisely that which stood highest hitherto: he who grasps *what* was destroyed there may look around to see if he still has anything at all left in his hands. Everything which until then was called "truth" is now recognized as the most harmful, spiteful, infernal form of falsehood; the holy pretext of "improving" mankind as a stratagem to suck out the life itself, to make it anemic. Morality as *vampirism*...He who unmasks the valuelessness of all the values which are or have been believed in; he no longer sees anything venerable in the most venerated type of men, even in those pronounced *holy*; he sees in them the most fateful kind of freaks, fateful *because they fascinate*...The concept God invented as the counter-concept to life — in it everything ruinous, poisonous, slanderous, the whole deadly enmity toward life brought together into one hideous unity! The concepts "other world," "true world" invented in order to devalue the *only* world there is — in order to leave no goal, no reason, no task remaining for our earthly reality! The concepts "soul," "spirit," at last even "immortal soul" invented in order to despise the body, in order to make it sick — "holy" — in order to display a horrible levity toward all those things which deserve to be taken seriously, questions of nutrition, housing, intellectual diet, treatment of the sick, cleanliness, and weather! Instead of soundness of health "salvation of the soul" — in other words, a *folie circulaire* between penitential convulsions and salvation hysteria! The concept "sin," together with the torture-instrument belonging to it, the concept "free will," invented in order to perplex the instincts, to render mistrust of the instincts as second nature! In the concept of the "selfless," the "self-denying one" the distinctive mark of *décadence*, the being *allured* by the injurious, the no longer being *able* to locate one's advantage, self-destruction turned generally into a sign of value, into "duty," into "holiness," into" the divine" in man! Finally — it is the most frightful of all — in the concept of the *good* man to side with all that is weak, sick, misdeveloped, suffering from itself, all *that which deserves to perish* — , the law of *selection* crossed, an ideal created out of the opposition to the proud and well-developed man, to the yea-saying man, to the man who is sure of his future, who guarantees the future — this man to be called the *evil* one from now on...And all this was believed in *as morality!* — Ecrasez l'infâme! — —

9

— Have I made myself understood? — *Dionysus versus the Crucified...*

THE ANTICHRIST

A CURSE ON CHRISTIANITY

Preface

This book belongs to the very few. Perhaps not one of them is even living yet. They may be the ones who understand my Zarathustra: how *could* I confuse myself with those who already get a hearing today? Only the day after tomorrow belongs to me. Some people are born posthumously.

The conditions under which one understands me, and then understands *of necessity* — I know them only too well. One must be honest and just in spiritual matters to the point of harshness in order to endure my seriousness, my passion. One must be used to living on mountains — to seeing the wretched prevailing chatter of politics and national self-seeking *beneath* oneself. One must be indifferent; one must never ask whether the truth is useful, whether it is fateful... A preference in strength for questions to which no one today has the courage; the courage for the *forbidden*, predestination for the labyrinth. An experience of seven solitudes. New ears for new music. New eyes for the furthest. A new conscience. A new conscience for truths which have hitherto remained mute. *And* the will to the economy of the grand style: keeping one's energy, one's *enthusiasm* in line... reverence for oneself; love for oneself; unconditional freedom towards oneself...

Well then! These alone are my readers, my true readers, my predestined readers: what do the *rest* matter? — The rest is merely mankind. — One must be above mankind in strength, in *loftiness* of soul — in contempt...

Friedrich Nietzsche

1

— Let us look each other in the face. We are Hyperboreans — we know well enough how far off the beaten paths we live. "Neither by land nor by sea will you find the way to the Hyperboreans": Pindar already knew that about us. Beyond north, ice, death — *our* life, *our* happiness... We have discovered happiness, we know the way, we have found the exit out of the labyrinth of thousands of years. Who *else* has found it? — Modern man perhaps? — "I know not where to turn; I am everything that knows not where to turn" — sighs modern man... From *this* modernity we became sick — from lazy peace, from cowardly compromising, from the whole virtuous uncleanliness of the modern Yes and No. This tolerance and *largeur* of the heart, which "forgives" all because it "understands" all, is sirocco for us. Better to live among ice than among modern virtues and other south winds! ... We were brave enough, we spared neither ourselves nor others: but for a long time we did not know *where to go* with our bravery. We became gloomy, we were called fatalists. *Our* fate — it lay in the fullness, the tension, the stowing away of our forces. We thirsted for lightning and deeds, we stayed farthest away from the happiness of weaklings, from "resignation" ... a thunderstorm was in our atmosphere, our nature grew dark — *for we had no path*. Formula for our happiness: a yes, a no, a straight line, a *goal*...

2

What is good? — Everything that heightens the feeling of power, the will to power, power itself in man. What is bad? — Everything that stems from weakness. What is happiness? — The feeling that power is *increasing* — that a resistance is overcome. *Not* contentment, but more power; *not* peace at all, but war; not virtue but proficiency (virtue in the Renaissance style, *virtu*, moraline–free virtue).

The weak and the misfits shall perish: first tenet of *our* love of man. And we should even help them to do so. What is more harmful than any vice? Active sympathy for all the misfits and the weak — Christianity...

3

The problem I herewith propose is not what shall succeed mankind in the sequence of living things (— man is an *end* —): but what type of man is to be *bred*, is to be *willed* as being higher in value, more worthy of life, more certain of a future.

This more valuable type has already existed often enough: but as a stroke of luck, as an exception, never as something *willed*. On the contrary, it was precisely *he* who was the most feared, he has hitherto almost been *the* frightful thing — and out of fear the opposite type has been willed, bred, *attained*: the domestic animal, the herd animal, the sick animal man — the Christian.

4

Mankind does *not* represent a development toward something better or stronger or higher in the way it is believed today. "Progress" is merely a modern idea, that is, a false idea. The European of today stands far below the European of the Renaissance; further development is *not* by any necessity at all an exaltation, an elevation, a strengthening.

In another sense there is a continuous success story of individual cases in the most various places and from the most various cultures in which a *higher type* does indeed appear: something which in relation to all of mankind is a kind of superman. Such lucky incidents of great success have always been possible and will perhaps always be possible. And even entire races, tribes, peoples can under certain circumstances bring off such a *lucky hit.*

5

One should not decorate and dress up Christianity: it has waged a *war to the death* against this *higher* type of man, it has placed all the fundamental instincts of this type under a ban, out of these instincts it has distilled evil, *the* evil one — the strong man as the typical reprobate, the "reprehensible man." Christianity has taken the side of all the weak, the base, the failures, it has made an ideal out of *opposition* to the preservative instincts of the strong life; it has ruined even the reason of the mentally strongest natures by teaching men to feel the highest values of the mind to be sinful, to be misleading, to be *temptations.* The most deplorable example: the corruption of Pascal, who believed in the corruption of his reason through original sin, while it had only been corrupted through his Christianity! —

6

It is a painful, a dreadful spectacle that has dawned upon me: I have drawn back the curtain from the *corruption* of man. This word, in my mouth, is protected at least from one suspicion: that it contains a moral accusation of man. It is meant to be — I would like to underline this once again — *moraline-free*: and this to the extent that I find that corruption precisely where people have hitherto aspired most consciously to "virtue," to "godliness." I understand corruption, as you may have already guessed, in the sense of *décadence*: my contention is that all the values which mankind now collects into its highest desideratum are *décadence values.*

I call an animal, a species, an individual corrupt when it has lost its instincts, when it chooses, when it *prefers*, what is detrimental to it. A history of the "higher feelings," of the "ideals of mankind" — and it is possible that I shall have to tell it — would almost be an explanation as well for *why* man is so corrupt. I think of life itself as the instinct for growth, for duration, for accumulation of strength, for *power*: where the will to power is lacking, there is decline. My contention is that all the values of mankind are *lacking* in this will — that values of decline, nihilistic values hold sway under the holiest of names.

7

Christianity is called the religion of *pity*. — Pity stands in opposition to the tonic emotions, which enhance the energy of the life-feeling: it brings about depression. One loses strength when one pities. Pity further increases and multiplies the loss of strength, which suffering-in-itself already brings into life. Suffering itself becomes contagious through pity; under certain circumstances a complete loss of life and life-energy can be reached which stands in an absurd relation to the quantity of the cause (— the case of the death of the Nazarene). That is the first viewpoint; but there is an even more important one. Supposing one measures pity by the value of the reactions it tends to bring forth, then its life-threatening character appears in a much clearer light. On the whole pity crosses the law of evolution, which is the law of *selection*. It preserves what is ripe for destruction, it defends life's disinherited and condemned through the abundance of misfits of all types, which it *keeps* alive, it gives life itself a gloomy and questionable aspect. Some have dared to call pity a virtue (— in every *noble* morality it passes for weakness —); they have gone further, they have made of it *the* virtue, the basis and source of all virtues — only, to be sure, keeping this always in mind, that it was from the viewpoint of a philosophy which was nihilistic, which inscribed *Denial of Life* on its shield. Schopenhauer was right about this: through pity life is denied, it is made *more worthy of denial* — pity is the *practice* of nihilism. To say it once more: this depressive and contagious instinct thwarts those instincts which exist for the preserving and value-enhancing of life: both as a multiplier of misery and as a *conservator* of all that is miserable it is a prime instrument for the advancement of *décadence* — pity persuades to *nothingness!* ... One does not say "nothingness": one says instead the "hereafter"; or "God"; or "*true* life"; or nirvana, salvation, blessedness... This innocent rhetoric from the domain of religio-moral idiosyncrasy immediately appears *much less innocent* once one perceives *which* tendency has wrapped itself in a mantle of sublime words here: the tendency which is *hostile to life*. Schopenhauer was hostile to life: *therefore* pity became a virtue for him. Aristotle, as we know, saw in pity a sick and dangerous condition which one would do well to get at now and then with a purgative: he thought of tragedy as a purgative: out of the instinct for life one would indeed be obliged to seek a means of puncturing such a sickly and dangerous accumulation of pity, as represented by the case of Schopenhauer (and unfortunately over whole literacy and artistic *décadence* as well, from St. Petersburg to Paris, from Tolstoy to Wagner): so that it might *burst*... Nothing is more unhealthy amidst our unhealthy modernity than Christian pity. To be a physician *here*, to be inexorable *here*, to wield the knife *here* — that belongs to *us*, that is *our* kind of love for mankind, with that *we* are philosophers, we Hyperboreans! — —

8

It is necessary to say *whom* we feel to be our opposition — the theologians and all that has theologian blood in its veins — our entire philosophy... One must have seen the catastrophe up close, better yet, one must nearly have perished from it, in order here to no longer think of it as a joke — (the free-thinking of our naturalists and physiologists is in my eyes a *joke* — the passion for these things is lacking in them, the *passion and suffering* from them —). This poisoning reaches much further than you think: I have found the theologian's instinctive arrogance wherever anyone today feels himself to be an *idealist* — wherever anyone assumes, by virtue of a higher origin, the right to cast strange and superior looks at reality... The idealist, just like the priest, holds all the great concepts in his hand (— and not only in his hand!), he plays them out with a benevolent contempt for "understanding," "senses," "honors," "science," he sees all these as *beneath* him, as destructive and seductive forces above which "the spirit" in pure for-itself-ness hovers — as if humility, chastity, poverty, *holiness*, in a word, had not done unspeakably more harm to life hitherto than any horrors or vice. The pure spirit is a pure lie... As long as the priest is still considered a *higher* type of man, that denier, slanderer, poisoner of life by *profession*, there is no answer to the question: what *is* truth? One already *has* stood truth on its head when the conscious advocate of nothing and negation is considered the representative of "truth"...

9

Against this theological instinct I wage war: I have found its tracks everywhere. Whoever has theological blood in his veins is from the start crooked and dishonorable toward all things. The pathos which develops out of this calls itself *faith*: closing one's eyes to oneself once and for all so as not to suffer at the sight of an incurable falsehood. One creates for oneself a moral, a virtue, a holiness out of the faulty perspective toward all things, one connects a good conscience with *false* seeing — one demands that no *other* kind of perspective shall have value anymore once one's own has been made sacrosanct with the names "God," "salvation," "eternity." I have dug up the theological instinct everywhere: it is the most widespread, truly *underground* form of falsehood there is on earth. Whatever a theologian feels to be true *must* be false: This is almost a criterion of truth. It is his deepest instinct of self-preservation, which forbids reality at any point from being respected, or even being spoken of. As far as theological influence extends, *value judgment* is stood on its head, the concepts "true" and "false" are necessarily reversed: what is most destructive to life is here called "true," what exalts, elevates, affirms, justifies, makes triumphant, that is called "false"... Should it happen that theologians, through the "conscience" of princes (or of peoples —), start stretching their hand out for *power*, let us not doubt *what* is basically happening every time: the will to the end, the *nihilistic* will wants power...

10

Among Germans I am understood immediately when I say that philosophy has been corrupted by theologian instinct. The Protestant pastor is the grandfather of German Philosophy, Protestantism itself its *peccatum originale.* Definition of Protestantism: the half-sided paralysis of Christianity — *and* of reason... One has only to say the words "Tübingen Seminary" to grasp *what* German philosophy is at bottom — a *cunning* theology... The Swabians are the best liars in Germany, they lie innocently... Why the rejoicing heard throughout the German academic world at the appearance of *Kant,* a world three-fourths composed of pastors' and teachers' sons — why the German conviction, which even today still finds an echo, that with Kant a change for the *better* was underway? The theologian instinct divined *what* now had become possible once again... A secret path to the old ideal stood open, the concept *"true* world," the concept of morality as the essence of the world (— the two most malevolent errors that there are!) were once more, thanks to a wily-clever skepticism, if not provable, then at least no longer *refutable...* Reason, the *right* of reason, does not extend so far... They had made out of reality an "appearance"; they had made a completely *fabricated* world, one of being, into reality... The success of Kant is merely a theologian's success: Kant was, like Luther, like Leibniz, one more impediment in the not so steady flow of German integrity — —

11

A word yet against Kant as a *moralist*. A virtue must be *our* discovery, *our* most personal self-defense and necessity: in every other sense it is merely a danger. What our life does not call for *harms* it: a virtue, which is merely a feeling of respect for the concept of "virtue," as Kant would have it, is harmful. "Virtue," "duty," "good-in-itself," good in the character of impersonality and universality — chimeras in which the decline, the final exhaustion of life, the Koenigsbergian Chinadom is expressed. The opposite is demanded by the deepest laws of preservation and growth: that everyone discover *his* virtue, his categorical imperative. A nation perishes when it confuses *its* duty with the concept of duty in general. Nothing ruins more deeply, more inwardly, than any "impersonal" duty, any sacrifice before the Moloch of abstraction. — That Kant's categorical imperative was not thought to be *dangerous to life!*... The theologian – instinct alone gave him protection! — An action to which life is compelled is proved to be a *correct* action by the pleasure it provides: and that nihilist with Christian-dogmatist bowels understood pleasure as an *objection*... What destroys more quickly than to work, to think, to feel without inner necessity, without a deep personal choice, without *pleasure*? As an automaton of "duty"? It is straightaway the *recipe* to *décadence*, to idiocy even... Kant became an idiot. — And this was the contemporary of *Goethe*! This fatal spider was considered the *German* philosopher — still is! I take care in saying what I think about the Germans... Did Kant not see in the French Revolution the transition from the inorganic form of the state to the *organic*? Did he not ask himself whether there had been an event which could be explained in no other way than by a moral predisposition on the part of mankind, so that with it the "tendency of mankind toward the good" would be proven once and for all? Kant's answer: "that is the Revolution." The erring instinct in each and every thing, *anti-nature* as instinct, German *décadence* as philosophy — *that is Kant!*

12

I except a few skeptics, the decent type in the history of philosophy: but the rest do not know the first requirements of intellectual integrity. They are like a bunch of little women, all these visionaries and prodigies — they take "beautiful feelings" for arguments, a "heaving bosom" for the bellows of divinity, conviction for a *criterion* of truth. In the end even Kant, in his "German" innocence, tried to make this form of corruption, this lack of intellectual conscience, into something scientific with the concept of "practical reason": he expressly invented a reason for the case in which one need not worry about reason, namely, when morality, when the sublime demand "thou shalt" makes itself known. If one considers that amongst almost all peoples the philosopher is only a further development of the priestly type, then this heirloom of the priest, this *counterfeiting before oneself*, is no longer surprising. If one has holy tasks such as improving, saving, redeeming man — if one carries divinity in one's bosom, is the mouthpiece for an otherworldly imperative, then with such a mission one already stands outside all merely reasonable valuations — already being sanctified *oneself* by such a task, already the type of a higher order *oneself!*... What does *science* matter to a priest! He is above that! — And the priest has *ruled* hitherto! *He has determined* the concepts "true" and "untrue"! ...

13

Let us not underestimate this: *we ourselves*, we free spirits, are already a "revaluation of all values," an *incarnate* declaration of war and victory on all the old concepts of "true" and "untrue." The most valuable insights are the last to be discovered; but *methods* are the most valuable insights. *All* the methods, *all* the presuppositions of our present scientific method have been opposed for thousands of years with the most profound contempt: on their account one was excluded from association with "honest" men — one was regarded as the "enemy of God," a "despiser of truth," "a man possessed." As a man of scientific character one was chandala... We have had the whole pathos of mankind against us — their concept of what truth *should* be, what the service of truth *should* be: every "thou shalt" hitherto has been directed *against* us... Our objectives, our practices, our quiet, cautious, mistrustful manner — all that seemed to them utterly unworthy and contemptible. — In the end one might reasonably ask whether it was not actually an *aesthetic* taste which kept mankind in blindness for so long: they desired from truth a *picturesque* effect, they desired in the same way from knowledge that it have a strong effect upon the senses. Our *modesty* offended their taste for the longest time... Oh, how well they divined that, these turkey-cocks of God — —

14

We have learned to think differently. We have become more modest in every respect. We no longer derive man from "spirit," from "divinity"; we have placed him back among the animals. We consider him the strongest animal, because he is the most cunning: his spirituality is a consequence thereof. On the other hand, we guard ourselves against a vanity, which also wants to make itself noticed again here — as if man were the great hidden design behind animal evolution. He is absolutely not the crown of creation: every creature is, next to him, at the same stage of perfection... And even in asserting this we are asserting too much: man is, relatively speaking, the most botched animal, the most morbid, the animal which has strayed most dangerously from its instincts — of course, with all that, also the most *interesting!* — As regards the animals, Descartes was the first who, with a boldness worthy of reverence, dared to think of the animal as a *machine*: our whole physiology strives to prove this proposition. Nor do we logically exclude man, as even Descartes did: what is generally understood about man today goes only just as far as his being understood mechanistically. Formerly man was given "free will" as his dowry from a higher order: today we have taken the will itself away from him, in the sense that will is no longer allowed to be understood as a faculty. The old word "will" serves only to designate a resultant, a sort of individual reaction which necessarily follows a host of partly contradictory, partly harmonious stimuli — the will "works" no more, "moves" no more... Formerly one saw in the consciousness of man, in his "spirit," the proof of his higher origin, his divinity: in order to *perfect* man he was advised to draw his senses back into himself like a tortoise, to cease all dealings with the earthly, laying aside the mortal frame: then the main part of him is left, the "pure spirit." We have thought better of this too: the development of consciousness, "spirit," strikes us precisely as a symptom of the relative imperfection of the organism, as a testing, groping, failing, as a toiling in which an unnecessarily large amount of nervous energy is used up. — We deny that anything can be made perfect as long as it is still made conscious. "Pure spirit" is pure stupidity: if in calculating we take away the nervous system and the senses, the "mortal frame," *then we miscalculate* — nothing more!...

15

In Christianity neither morality nor religion makes contact with reality at any point. Nothing but imaginary *causes* ("God," "soul," "I," "spirit," "free will" — or else "unfree will"; nothing but imaginary *effects* ("sin," "redemption," "grace," "punishment," "forgiveness of sins"). An intercourse between imaginary *beings* ("God," "spirits," "souls"); an imaginary *natural* science (anthropocentric; complete lack of the concept of natural causes); an imaginary *psychology* (nothing but self-misunderstanding, interpretations of pleasant or unpleasant general feelings, for example the condition of the *nervus sympathicus*, with the aid of the sign language of the religio-moral idiosyncrasy — "repentance," "pangs of conscience," "temptation by the devil," "the closeness of God"; an imaginary *teleology* ("the Kingdom of God," "the Last Judgment," "eternal life"). This world of *pure fiction* is distinguished from the world of dreams, very much to its disadvantage, by the fact that the latter *mirrors* reality, while *it* falsifies, devalues, denies reality. Once the concept "Nature" was invented as a counter-concept to "God," "natural" had to become the word for "reprehensible" — that whole fictional world had its roots in hatred for the natural (— for reality! —), it is the expression of a deep discontent with the actual... *But with this everything is explained.* Who alone has reasons *to lie his way* out of reality? He who *suffers* from it. But to suffer from reality means to be a *failed* reality... The predominance of feelings of displeasure over feelings of pleasure is the *first cause* for a fictitious morality and religion: such a predominance, however, provides the *formula* for *décadence*...

16

A critique of the *Christian concept of God* necessitates the same conclusion. — A people that still believes in itself still has its own God too. In him it reveres the conditions through which it has come out on top, his virtues, — it projects its delight in itself, its feeling of power, into a being one can give thanks to. He who is rich wants to *deliver up*; a proud people needs a God, in order to *offer up*... Religion, within such presuppositions, is a form of thankfulness. One is thankful for oneself: for that one needs a God. — Such a God must be able to be useful and harmful, must be able to be friend or foe — one admires him in good as well as in bad. The *unnatural* castration of a God into a God merely of the good would lie outside all things desirable here. One has as much need of the evil God as of the good: one should be thankful for the whole of one's existence, not just for tolerance and human kindness. Of what consequence would a God be who knew nothing of wrath, revenge, envy, scorn, cunning, violent acts? who had perhaps not once known the enraptured *ardeurs* of victory and annihilation? One would not understand such a God: why should one have him? — To be sure: when a nation is going to ruin; when it feels its faith in the future, its hope of freedom, finally disappear; when submissiveness is first in usefulness, when the virtues of the subjugated become the conditions for survival, then it *must* also change its God. He now becomes a dissembler, fearful, unassuming, counseling "peace of soul," hating-no-more, forbearance, "love" even toward friend and foe. He moralizes continually, he crawls into the hole of every private virtue, becomes the God for everyman, becomes a private person, a cosmopolitan... Formerly he represented a people, the strength of a people, all things aggressive and thirsting for power out of a people: now he is merely just the good God... In fact, there is no other alternative for gods: *either* they are the will to power — and as long as they are they will be the people's gods — *or* else the will-lessness to power — and then they necessarily become *good*...

17

When the will to power declines in any form, there is every time as well a physiological regression, a *décadence*. The divinity of *décadence*, pruned of its manliest virtues and drives, necessarily becomes henceforth the God of the psychologically withdrawn, the weak. They do *not* call themselves the weak; they call themselves "the good"... One can grasp, without any further hint, at which moment in history the dualistic fiction of a good and evil God first became possible. With the same instinct by which the subjugated reduce their God to "the good in itself," they rub out the good qualities from the God of their conquerors: they take revenge on their masters by making their masters' God *turn devil*. — *The good* God, just the same as the devil: both offspring of *décadence*. How can one today still defer so much to the simplicity of Christian theologians to decree along with them that the onward development of the concept of God from "the God of Israel," the people's God, to the Christian God, the epitome of all things good, represents an *advance*? — But even Renan does this. As if Renan had a right to simplicity! The opposite stares one in the face, I dare say.

When the preconditions of *ascending* life, when everything strong, brave, masterful, proud has been eliminated from the concept of God, when he sinks down step by step into the symbol of a staff for the weary, into a sheet anchor for all who are drowning, when he becomes the poor man's God, the sinners' God, the God of the sick *par excellence*, and the title "Savior," "Redeemer" is as it were left *over* as the title of divinity per se: *of what* does such a transformation speak? Such a reduction of the divine? — To be sure: "the kingdom of God" has become enlarged thereby. Formerly he had only his people, his "chosen" people. In the meantime he has gone a-wandering, into foreign parts, just like his people; since then he has sat still nowhere: till at last he felt at home everywhere, the great cosmopolitan — till he had "the great majority" and half the earth on his side. But the God of the "great majority," the democrat among gods became no proud pagan God in spite of this: he remained a Jew, he remained the nook and cranny God, the God of all dark corners and places, of all unhealthy quarters throughout the whole world! ... His worldwide kingdom is now as before an underworld-kingdom, a hospital, a *souterrain* kingdom, a ghetto-kingdom... And he himself, so pale, so weak, so *décadent* ... Even the palest of the pale were still able to become master over him, the gentlemen metaphysicians, the concept-albinos. They spun their webs around him so long that he, hypnotized by their movements, became himself a spider, a metaphysician. Henceforth he spun the world again out of himself — *sub specie Spinozae* — henceforth he transfigured himself into something ever thinner and paler, became an "ideal," became "pure spirit," became "*absolutum*," became the "thing-in-itself" ... *Downfall of a God*: God became the "thing-in-itself"...

18

The Christian concept of God — God as God of the sick, God as spider, God as spirit — is one of the most corrupt conceptions of God ever attained on earth; perhaps it even represents the low-water mark in the descending development of the god-type. God degenerated into the *contradiction of life* instead of being its transfiguration and eternal *yea*! In God a declaration of war against life, nature, and the will to life! God the formula for every slander of "this world," for every lie about "that world"! In God nothingness deified, the will to nothingness sanctified! ...

19

That the strong races of northern Europe did not cast aside the Christian God certainly does no credit to their religious talent — not to speak of their taste. They *ought* to have been finished with such a sickly and decrepit offspring of *décadence*. But a curse lies upon them for not being finished with it: they have taken up the sickness, the old age, the contradiction in all their instincts — since then they have not created another God! Almost two thousand years and not a single new God! But ever still, and as if existing by right, as if the *ultimatum* and *maximum* of the God-shaping force, of the *creator spiritus* in man, this miserable God of Christian monotono-theism! This hybrid creation of decline composed of naught, concept, and contradiction, in which all the instincts of *décadence*, all cowardliness and weariness of soul have their sanction! — —

20

With my condemnation of Christianity I should not like to have committed an injustice toward a related religion which even outweighs it in the number of its believers: *Buddhism*. Both belong together as nihilistic religions — they are *décadence*-religions — , both are separated from each other in the strangest way. That one may now *compare* them, the critic of Christianity is deeply obliged to the Indian scholars. — Buddhism is a hundred times more realistic than Christianity — it has the inheritance of cool and objective problem-posing in its blood, it comes *after* a philosophical movement lasting hundreds of years: the concept of "God" is already abolished when it comes. Buddhism is the only really *positivistic* religion history has to offer us, even in its epistemology (a strict phenomenalism —), it no longer says "the struggle against *sin*," but quite in keeping with reality, "the struggle against *suffering*." It has — this distinguishes it profoundly from Christianity — the self-deceit of moral concepts already behind it — it stands, expressed in my language, *beyond* good and evil. — The *two* physiological facts upon which it rests and fixes its eye are: *first,* an excessive sensitivity of sensibility which expresses itself as a refined capacity for pain, *then* an over-intellectuality, an all-too-long living amid concepts and logical procedures under which the personal instinct has sustained damage to the advantage of the "impersonal" (— both of them conditions which at least some of my readers, the objective" ones, will know from experience, as I do). By virtue of these physiological conditions a state of *depression* has arisen: against this Buddha takes hygienic measures. He employs life in the open against it, the wandering life; moderation and selection in eating fare; caution towards all spirituous liquors, caution as well towards all emotions which produce gall, which heat the blood; no *worry*, either for oneself or for others. He requires ideas which produce repose or enliven — he invents means of weaning oneself from the others. He understands goodness, being goodly, as health-promoting. Prayer is barred, as is *asceticism*; no categorical imperative, no *coercion* in general, even within the monastic community (— one can get out again —). All these would only mean a strengthening of that excessive sensitivity. For the same reason he also demands no struggle against those who think otherwise; his teaching resists nothing *more* than the feeling of revenge, antipathy, *ressentiment* (— "not through enmity is enmity ended": the stirring refrain of the whole of Buddhism...). And rightfully so: precisely these emotions would be *unhealthy* in view of the chief dietetic design. Against the spiritual weariness he finds and which expresses itself in an all-too-great "objectivity" (that is, the weakening of individual interest, loss of center of gravity, of "egoism"), he fights with a strict guidance of even the most spiritual interests back to the *person*. In the teaching of Buddha egoism becomes a duty: the "one thing is necessary," the "how do *you* get free of suffering" regulates and circumscribes the whole spiritual diet (— one may perhaps recall that Athenian who likewise waged war against pure "scientific-ness," Socrates, who raised personal egoism to a morality even in the realm of problems).

21

Buddhism presupposes a very mild climate, a great gentleness and liberality in customs, *no* militarism; and that it is the higher and even learned classes in which the movement has its home. The highest goal is cheerfulness, stillness, freedom from desire, and this goal is *attained.* Buddhism is no religion in which one merely aspires to perfection: perfection is the normal case. —

In Christianity the instincts of the subjugated and suppressed come to the fore: the lowest classes seek their salvation in it. Here the casuistry of sin, self-criticism, conscience-inquisition is practiced as an *occupation*, a specific against boredom; here an emotion toward a *mighty one* named "God" is constantly maintained (through prayer); here the highest is regarded as unattainable, as a gift, as "grace." Here the public act is also lacking; the hiding place, the dark room is Christian. Here the body is despised, hygiene rejected as sensuality: the Church even defends itself against cleanliness (— the first Christian measure after the expulsion of the Moors was the closing of the public baths, of which Cordova alone possessed two hundred and seventy). Christian in a certain sense means cruelty towards oneself and others; hatred towards those who think otherwise; the will to persecute. Gloomy and upsetting ideas are at the fore; the most highly desired states, designated by the highest names, are epileptoid; the diet is so chosen as to favor morbid phenomena and over-excite the nerves. Christian means mortal enmity towards the lords of the earth, towards the "noble" — and at the same time a sly, secretive rivalry (— one leaves them the "body," one wants *only* the "soul"...). Christian means hatred of the *spirit*, of pride, courage, freedom, *libertinage* of the spirit; Christian means hatred of the *senses*, of joy in the senses, of joy in general...

22

Christianity, when it left its original soil, the lowest classes, the *underworld* of the ancient world, when it set out after power among barbarian peoples, here it no longer presupposed *weary* men, but inwardly savage and self-lacerating ones — strong men but misfits. Here dissatisfaction with oneself, suffering from oneself, is *not* as it is with the Buddhists, an excessive sensitivity and capacity for feeling pain, but on the contrary an overwhelming desire for painmaking, for the release of inner tension in hostile actions and conceptions. Christianity needed *barbaric* concepts and values in order to become master over barbarians: some of these include sacrifice of the first-born, blood-drinking at communion (the Lord's Supper), contempt for intellect and for culture; torture in all forms, sensual and non-sensual; the great pomp of public worship. Buddhism is a religion for late individuals, for races that have become kindly, gentle, over-intellectual, that feel pain too easily (— Europe will not be ripe for it for a long time yet —): it is a return back to peace and cheerfulness for them, to a diet in the spiritual, to a certain hardening in the corporal. Christianity wants to be master over *beasts of prey*; its method is to make them *sick* — weakening is the Christian recipe for *taming*, for "civilization." Buddhism is a religion for the conclusion and weariness of a civilization; Christianity finds no civilization as yet — in some cases it lays the foundation for one.

23

Buddhism, to say it again, is a hundred times colder, more truthful, more objective. It no longer finds it necessary to make its suffering, its capacity for pain, *respectable* to itself through the interpretation of sin — it simply says what it thinks, "I suffer." To the barbarian, on the other hand, suffering in itself is nothing respectable: he first needs an explanation in order to admit to himself *that* he is suffering (his instinct directs him rather toward denial of his suffering, toward silent endurance). Here the word "devil" was a favor: one had an overpowering and frightening enemy — one need not be ashamed of suffering at the hands of such an enemy. —

Christianity has some fine points in its first principles which belong to the Orient. Above all it knows that in itself it is a matter of complete indifference whether something is true, but of the highest importance as far as whether it is believed to be true. The truth and the *belief* that something is true: two completely separate worlds of interest, worlds of *opposition* almost — one comes to one and the other by fundamentally different paths. To be knowledgeable in this — this nearly *makes* a wise man in the Orient: so the Brahmins understand it, so Plato understands it, so every student of esoteric wisdom does. If, for example, there is some *happiness* in believing oneself redeemed from sin, then the prerequisite is *not* necessary that man be sinful but that he *feel* sinful. But if in general faith above all is necessary, then reason, knowledge, and inquiry are discredited: the way to truth becomes the *forbidden* way. — Strong *hope* is a much greater *stimulant* of life than any single genuinely occurring bit of happiness. Sufferers must be sustained by a hope, which cannot be gainsaid by any reality — which is not abolished by any fulfillment: a hope in the beyond. (Precisely because of this capacity for keeping the unhappy in suspense, hope was regarded by the Greeks as the evil of evils, the only actually *malicious* evil: it remained behind in the box of evils.) — So that *love* is possible, God must be a person; so that the lowest instincts can have their say, God must be young. For the ardor of the women a beautiful saint is pushed into the foreground, for the men a Mary. This under the presupposition that Christianity wants to be master on a soil where aphroditic or Adonis cults have already determined the concept of religious worship. The requirement of *chastity* increases the vehemence and inwardness of the religious instinct — it makes the worship warmer, more enthusiastic, more soulful. — Love is the condition wherein man sees things most as they are *not*. The illusory power is here at its height, as is the sweetening, the *transfiguring* power. In love one endures more than otherwise, one bears all. A religion had to be found in which love is possible: with that one is beyond the worst in life — one no longer sees it at all. — So much for the three Christian virtues of faith, hope and love: I call them the three Christian *shrewdnesses*. — Buddhism is too late, too positivistic, to ever be shrewd in this way. —

24

I only touch on the problem of the *origin* of Christianity here. The *first* sentence in its solution is: Christianity can only be understood in terms of the soil from which it grew — it is *not* a counter-movement against the Jewish instinct, it is its logical consequence itself, a step further in its awe-inspiring logic. In the formula of the Savior: "Salvation is of the Jews." — The second sentence is: the psychological type of the Galilean is still recognizable, but only in its complete degeneration (which is at the same time a mutilation and an overloading with foreign traits) could it serve the purpose for which it was created — as the type of the *Savior* of mankind. —

The Jews are the strangest people in the history of the world because, faced with the question of being or not being, they preferred, with a completely uncanny awareness, being *at any price:* this price was the radical *falsification* of all nature, all naturalness, all reality, the whole inner world as well as the outer. They disassociated themselves *from* all conditions under which a people had hitherto been able to live, been *permitted* to live; they created out of themselves a counter-concept to *natural* conditions — they twisted around religion, religious worship, morality, history, psychology, one after the other, in an irreparable way, into the *contradiction of their natural values*. We meet the same phenomenon once more and in unspeakably larger proportions, though only as a copy — the Christian Church is, compared to "the nation of the holy ones," without any claim to originality. Along with this, the Jews are the most *fateful* nation in the history of the world: by their after-effect they have played mankind false to such a degree that even today the Christian can feel anti-Jewish without himself realizing that he is the *ultimate consequence of the Jews.*

In my "Genealogy of Morals" I introduced for the first time psychologically the concept of opposition between a *noble* morality and a *ressentiment*-morality, the latter derived *from a denial* of the former: but this is the Judeo-Christian morality completely. In order to say no to all that represents on earth the *ascending* movement of life, power, beauty, successfulness, self-affirmation, here the genius-become-instinct of *ressentiment* had to invent for itself *another* world from which that same *life-affirmation* would appear as the evil one, as the reprehensible-in-itself. Psychologically re-reckoned, the Jewish people are a people of the toughest vitality who, placed under impossible conditions, voluntarily, out of the deepest shrewdness of self-preservation, took the side of all *décadence* instincts — not as being ruled by them but because they divined in them a power with which one can prevail *against* "the world." The Jews are the antithesis of all *décadents:* they have had to *represent* them to the point of illusion, they have known, with a *non plus ultra* of histrionic genius, how to place themselves at the head of all *décadence* movements (— such as the Christianity of *Paul* —) in order to create something out of them stronger than any *yea-saying* party of life. For the type of man longing for power in Judaism and Christianity, the *priestly* type, *décadence* is only a *means:* this type of man has a life-interest in making man *sick* and in twisting around the concepts "good" and "evil," "true" and "false" in a life-endangering and world-slandering sense. —

25

The history of Israel is invaluable as the typical history of all *denaturalization* of natural values: I shall point out five facts in the same process. Originally, above all in the time of the kingdom, Israel also stood in the *correct*, that is to say, in the natural, relation to all things. Its Yahweh was the expression of power-consciousness, joy in oneself, hope for oneself: in Him one expected victory and prosperity, with Him one trusted in Nature, that she would give what the people found necessary — above all, rain. Yahweh is the God of Israel and *consequently* the God of justice: the logic of every people that is in power and has a good conscience about it. In festival ritual these two sides of a people's self-affirmation find expression: they are grateful for the immense destiny through which they have come out on top, they are grateful in relation to the yearly course of seasons and to all good fortune in cattle breeding and agriculture. — This state of affairs long remained the ideal, even after it was done away with in a sorrowful fashion: anarchy from within, the Assyrian from without. But as the highest desideratum the people held on to that vision of a king who is a good soldier and a strict judge: above all, that typical prophet (that means critic and satirist of the moment) Isaiah. — But that hope remained unfulfilled. The old God no longer *could* do what he once could. He should have been let go. What happened? They *changed* their concept of Him — they *denaturalized* their concept of Him: at this price they held on to Him. — Yahweh the God of "justice" — *no longer* one with Israel, an expression of national self-respect: only a God under certain conditions ... The concept of Him becomes a tool in the hands of priestly agitators who henceforth interpret all good fortune as reward, all misfortune as punishment for disobedience toward God, as "sin": that most mendacious mode of interpretation of an alleged "moral world order," with which, once and for all, the natural conception of "cause" and "effect" is stood on its head. When one has first removed natural causality from the world by means of reward and punishment, then one requires an *unnatural* causality: all the rest of the unnaturalness follows thereafter. A God who *demands* — in place of a God who helps, who devises means, who is at bottom the word for every happy inspiration of courage and self-confidence... Morality no longer the expression of the living and growing conditions of a people, no longer its deepest instinct of life, but become abstract, become something opposed to life — morality as the fundamental degradation of the imagination, as the "evil eye" for all things. *What* is Jewish, *What* is Christian morality? Chance robbed of its innocence; misfortune besmirched with the concept of "sin"; well-being as danger, as "temptation"; physiological indisposition poisoned by the worm of conscience ...

26

The concept of God falsified; the moral concept falsified — the Jewish priesthood did not stop there. The whole *history* of Israel was of no use: away with it! These priests brought about that miracle of falsification as their document, and it lies before us in a good part of the Bible: with unequaled scorn toward every tradition, every historical reality, they *translated into religious terms* their own national past, that is, they made of it a stupid salvation-mechanism of guilt toward Yahweh and punishment, of piety toward Yahweh and reward. We would have felt this most shameful act of historical falsification much more painfully if thousands of years of the *ecclesiastical* interpretation had not made us almost insensible to the demands of integrity *in historicis.* And the Church was seconded by the philosophers: the *lie* of the "moral world order" pervades the whole development of even the newer philosophy. What does "moral world order" mean? That there is, once and for all, a will of God as to what man is to do and what he is not to do; that the value of a people, of an individual himself, is measured according to how much or how little the will of God is obeyed; that in the fate of a people, in an individual himself, the will of God proves to be *commanding,* that is, punishing and rewarding, according to the degree of obedience. — The *reality* instead of this pitiful lie is: a parasitical kind of man that thrives at the expense of all healthy forms of life, the *priest,* misuses the name of God: he calls a condition of society in which the priest determines the value of things the "kingdom of God"; he calls the means by virtue of which such a condition is attained or maintained the will of God"; with a cold-blooded cynicism he measures the peoples, the times, the individuals according to whether they availed themselves of the priestly supremacy or whether they opposed it. One should see them at work: in the hands of the Jewish priests the *great* era in the history of Israel became an era of decay, the Exile; the long misfortune was transformed into an eternal *punishment* for the great era — an era in which the priest was nothing yet. In accordance with requirements they made poor grovelers and grumblers or "godless ones" out of the mighty, *very freely* made figures of Israel's history, they simplified the psychology of every great event into the idiotic formula of obedience *or* disobedience toward God." A step further: the "will of God" (that is to say, the conditions for the preservation of priestly power) must be *known* — *to this end a "revelation"* is required. In plain English: a great literary forgery becomes necessary, a "Holy Scripture" is discovered — it is made public with all hieratic pomp, with days of penitence and cries of lamentation over the long sinfulness. The "will of God" had stood fast for the longest time: the whole disaster lay in their having become estranged from the "Holy Scriptures"... The "will of God" had already been revealed to Moses... What had happened? The priest had, with severity, with pedantry, right down to the rates great and small he was to be paid (— not forgetting the tastiest pieces of meat: for the priest is a beefsteak-eater), formulated once and for all *what he wants to have*, what the will of God is"... From now on the things of life are so ordered that the priest is *everywhere indispensable*; at all natural occurrences in life, birth, marriage, sickness, death, to say nothing of "offerings" (meal-times), the holy parasite appears in order to *denaturalize* them — in his language: to "sanctify"... For one must understand this: every natural custom, every natural institution (state, justice administration, marriage, care for the sick and the poor), every summons delivered by the instinct of life, in short, everything that has its value *in itself*, is made fundamentally worthless, adverse to value through the parasitism of the priest (or the moral "world order"): a sanction is subsequently required — a *value-bestowing*

126

power is necessary, one which denies the nature within and precisely with this first *creates* a value ... The priest de-values, *de-sanctifies* nature: it is at this price he continues to exist at all. — Disobedience toward God, that is, toward the priest, toward "the Law" now receives the name of "sin"; the means for one's "reconciling with God" again are, as stands to reason, means by which subjection to the priest is even more thoroughly guaranteed: the priest alone "saves"... Psychologically re-reckoned, "sins" become indispensable to any society organized by priests: they are the actual handles of power, the priest *lives* on sins, for him it is necessary that sins be "committed" ... Highest precept: "God forgives those who do penance" — in plain English: *those who subject themselves to the priest.*

27

On a soil *false* to this degree, where all nature, all natural value, all *reality* had the deepest instincts of the ruling class against it, *Christianity* grew up, a form of deadly enmity to reality as yet unsurpassed. The "holy people" that had retained only priestly values, only priestly words, for all things, and with a conclusive logical consistency capable of inspiring fear had cut themselves off from everything else powerful on earth, deeming it "unholy," "world," "sin" — this people produced for its instinct a final formula which was logical to the point of self-negation: it *negated*, as *Christianity*, the last form of reality yet, the "holy people," the "Chosen People," the *Jewish* reality itself. The case is first-rate: the small rebellious movement baptized with the name of Jesus of Nazareth, is the Jewish instinct *once more* — in other words, the priestly instinct which can no longer endure the priest as reality, the discovery of an even *more abstract* form of being, an even *more unreal* vision of the world than the organization of a church stipulates. Christianity *negates* the Church... I fail to see against what the rebellion was directed whose originator Jesus is understood or *misunderstood* to be if it was not the rebellion against the Jewish church — "church" taken exactly in the sense we take the word today. It was a rebellion against "the good and the just," against the "holy men of Israel," against the hierarchy of society — *not* against its corruption, but against caste, privilege, order, formula; it was disbelief in the "higher men," the *No* spoken against all that was priest and theologian. But the hierarchy which was called into question with this, even if only for a moment, was the building on stilts upon which the Jewish people still continued to exist at all amidst the "waters" — the laboriously obtained *last* possibility of remaining, the residue of their special existence: an attack on them was an attack on the deepest national instinct, on the toughest national life-will that has ever existed on earth. This holy anarchist who summoned the lower classes, the outcasts and "sinners," the *chandala* within Jewry, to oppose the ruling order — in a language, if the Gospels are to be trusted, which even today would lead to Siberia — was a political criminal, in just so far as would be possible in an *absurdly unpolitical* community. This brought him to the cross: the proof for this is the inscription on the cross. He died for *his* guilt — all basis is lacking, no matter how often it is asserted, that he died for the guilt of others. —

28

It is another question completely whether he had any such opposition in mind at all — whether he was not merely *felt* to be this opposition. And here I first touch on the problem of the *psychology of the savior.* — I confess that few books I read have such difficulties as the Gospels do. These difficulties are other than those upon whose proof the learned curiosity of the German intellect celebrated one of its most unforgettable triumphs. The time is long gone since I, too, like every young scholar fully enjoyed with the clever slowness of the refined philologist, the work of the incomparable Strauss. At that time I was twenty years old: now I am too serious for that. What do I care about contradictions in the "tradition"? How can saints' legends be called "tradition" at all! The histories of saints are the most ambiguous literature there generally is: to apply the scientific method on them, *when no other documents exist*, appears to me to be condemned from the start — merely learned idleness...

29

What matters to *me* is the psychological type of the savior. He *could* indeed be contained in the Gospels in spite of the Gospels, however much mutilated or overloaded with alien traits: as Francis of Assisi is preserved in his legends in spite of his legends. *Not* the truth concerning what he did, what he said, how he actually died: but the question whether he is still conceivable at all, whether he has "come down to us." The attempts I know of to extract even the *history* of a "soul" from the Gospels seem to me proof of an abominable psychological light-mindedness. Mr. Renan, that buffoon *in psychologicis*, has introduced the two most *improper* concepts possible into his explanation of the Jesus type: the concept of the *genius* and the concept of the *hero* ("*héros*"). But if anything is unevangelical, it is the concept of the hero. Precisely the opposite of all struggling, of all feeling-oneself-in-battle has here become instinct: the incapacity for resistance here becomes morality ("Resist not evil!" the deepest utterance of the Gospels, the key to them in a certain sense), blessedness in peace, in meekness, in the *inability* to be an enemy. What does "glad tidings" mean? True life, eternal life has been found, — it is not promised, it is here, it is within *you*: as a life in love, in love without deduction or exemption, without distance. Everyone is the child of God — Jesus demands absolutely nothing for himself alone — , as a child of God everyone is equal to everyone else ... To make a *hero* out of Jesus! — and what an utter misunderstanding of the word "genius"! Our whole concept, our cultural concept of "spirit" makes no sense at all in the world in which Jesus lived. Spoken with the strictness of an physiologist, an entirely different word would rather be in place here: the word idiot. We recognize a condition of morbid susceptibility in the *sense of touch* which recoils in horror at every contact, every grasp of a solid object. One translates such a physiological *habitus* into its ultimate logic — as the instinctive hatred toward *every* reality, as flight into the "unintelligible," the "incomprehensible," as ill-will toward every form, every concept of time and space, toward all that is solid, custom, institution, church, as being at home in a world which no kind of reality stirs any longer, an "inner world" only, a "true" world, an "eternal" world ... "The kingdom of God is *within you*" ...

30

The instinctive hatred toward reality: consequence of an extreme capacity for irritation and injury which no longer wants to be "touched" because it feels every touch too deeply.

The instinctive exclusion of all aversion, all enmity, all boundaries and distances in feeling: consequence of an extreme capacity for irritation and injury which already feels any resistance, any having to resist, as unbearable *displeasure* (that is, as *destructive*, as *ill-advised* by the instinct of self-preservation) and knows bliss (pleasure) only in offering resistance no more, to no one anymore, neither to evil nor the evil-doer — love as the sole, as the *last* life-possibility ...

These are the two *physiological realities* upon which, out of which, the redemption doctrine has grown. I call it a sublime further development of hedonism upon a thoroughly morbid basis. Most nearly related to it, though with a large additional supply of Greek vitality and nervous energy, is Epicureanism, the redemption doctrine of paganism. Epicurus is a *typical décadent*: first recognized by me as such. — The fear of pain, even of the infinitesimal in pain — it *cannot* end any other way than in a *religion of love* ...

31

I have given my answer to the problem beforehand. The presupposition for it is that the type of the redeemer is preserved for us only in a strongly distorted form. This distortion has a lot of plausibility to it: for several reasons such a type could not remain pure, whole, free from ornamentation. The milieu in which this strange figure moved must have left its mark upon him, and even more so the history, the *destiny* of the first Christian community: out of this the type grew, retrospectively enriched with traits which only become comprehensible in terms of war and propaganda aims. That strange and sick world to which the Gospels introduce us — a world like that of a Russian novel in which the dregs of society, nervous disorder, and "childlike" idiocy seem to be making a rendezvous — , must, in any event, have *coarsened* the type: the first disciples, in particular, had to translate a being completely immersed in symbols and incomprehensibilities into their own crudity in order to get anything out of it at all, — only after shaping it into more recognizable forms was the type *existent* for them... The prophet, the Messiah, the future judge, the moral teacher, the miracle man, John the Baptist — just so many opportunities for misjudging the type ... Let us not underestimate the *proprium* of all great, in particular, sectarian veneration: it effaces the original, often painfully unfamiliar traits and idiosyncrasies of the revered being — *it does not even see them.* One has to regret that no Dostoyevsky lived in the neighborhood of this most interesting *décadent*, I mean someone who had just the right feel for the touching appeal of such a mixture of the sublime, the sick, and the child-like. One final viewpoint: the type, as a *décadence* type, could actually have been of a curious multiplicity and contradictoriness: such a possibility is not to be completely ruled out. Nevertheless, everything speaks against it: the very tradition in this case would have to have been remarkably true and objective: whereof we have reasons for assuming the opposite. In the meantime a contradiction yawns between the mountain-, lake-, and meadow-preacher, whose appearance is like a Buddha on a soil very little like India, and that fanatic of assault, mortal enemy of theologian and priest, whom Renan's malice has extolled as "le grand maitre en ironie." I myself do not doubt that the plentiful mass of gall (and even of *esprit*) first overflowed into the type of the Master on account of the agitated condition of Christian propaganda: one knows very well indeed the unthinkable behavior of all sectarians in arranging for themselves out of their maker their own *apologie*. When the first community stood in need of a judging, wrangling, raging, maliciously hair-splitting theologian *opposed* to theologians, they created for themselves their "God" according to their requirements: just as they put into his mouth without hesitation those completely un-evangelistic concepts which now they could not do without, "Second Coming," "Last Judgment," every kind of temporal expectation and promise. —

32

I resist, to say it once again, the carrying over of the fanatic into the type of the savior: the word *imperieux* alone, which Renan uses, already *annuls* the type. The "glad tidings" are precisely that there are no more opposites; the kingdom of heaven belongs to the *children*; the faith that is made known here is not a faith gained by struggle — it is, as it were, a return to childlike manners in the spiritual. The case of delayed and underdeveloped puberty in the organism, as a consequence of degeneration, is at least familiar to the physiologists. — Such a faith does not get angry, does not rebuke, does not resist: it does not bring "the sword" — it has no idea at all to what extent it could cause dissension one day. It does not prove itself, either through miracle or through reward and promise, even less still "through the Scriptures": it is every moment its own miracle, its own proof, its own "kingdom of God." This faith does not formulate itself either — it *lives*, it resists formulas. To be sure, chance determines the environment, the language, the preparatory training for a certain sphere of concepts: primitive Christianity handled *only* Jewish–Semitic concepts "(— eating and drinking at the Lord's Supper belong here, that concept so badly misused by the church, like all things Jewish). But one should take care not to see more than sign language in this, semiotics, an opportunity for similes. Precisely that no word of his be taken literally is the preliminary condition for this anti-realist to be able to speak at all. Among Indians the Sankhya concepts would have served him, among Chinese those of Lao-tse — and without feeling any difference thereby. — One could, with some freedom of expression, call Jesus a "free spirit" — he cares nothing for all things fixed: the word *kills*, all that is fixed *kills*. The concept, the *experience* of "life" as he alone knows it, opposes every kind of word, formula, law, faith, dogma. He speaks only of the innermost: "life" or "truth" or "light" is his word for the innermost — everything else, all of reality, all of nature, language itself, has for him merely the value of a sign, a simile. — One must make absolutely no mistake at this point, no matter how great a temptation there may be in the Christian, that is, the *ecclesiastical* prejudice: such a symbolist *par excellence* stands outside all religion, all notions of cult, all history, all natural science, all world experience, all knowledge, all polities, all psychology, all books, all art — his "knowledge" is just *pure folly* over the fact *that* the like of these things exist. Not even by hearsay is he acquainted with *culture*, he has no need to fight against it — he does not deny it ... The same goes for the *state*, for the whole civic order and society, for *work*, for war — he never had reason to deny "the world," he had no notion of the church concept "world"... *Denial* is precisely what is quite impossible for him — . In the same way dialectic is lacking, the idea for it is lacking that a belief, a "truth," could be proved by reasons (— *his* proofs are inner "lights," inner pleasurable sensations and self-affirmations, nothing but "proofs of strength" —). Nor *can* such a doctrine contradict: it does not comprehend at all that other doctrines exist, *can* exist; it cannot imagine a contrary opinion at all... Where it encounters one, it will, with innermost compassion, grieve over the "blindness" — for it sees the "light" — , but make no objection...

33

In the whole psychology of the "Gospel" the concept of guilt and punishment is absent; likewise the concept of reward. "Sin," any comparative distance between God and man is done away with — *precisely this is the glad tidings.*" Eternal bliss is not promised, it is not tied to conditions: it is the *only* reality — the rest is symbol, in order to speak of it... The *consequence* of such a condition projects itself into a *new practice*, the actual evangelical practice. A "belief" is not what distinguishes the Christian: the Christian acts, he is distinguished by a *different* sort of action. That he offers no resistance to the one who does him evil, neither in word nor in his heart. That he makes no difference between foreign and domestic, between Jew and non-Jew "one's neighbor," properly speaking, one's fellow-believer, the Jew). That he grows angry towards no one, looks down on no one. That he neither appears in courts of law nor makes a claim there ("not swearing"). That under no circumstances does he separate from his wife, not even in the case of the wife's proven unfaithfulness. — All at bottom *one* rule, all consequences of *one* instinct. —

The life of the Savior was nothing other than *this* practice — his death was also nothing else... He no longer required any formulas, any rites in his dealings with God — not even prayer. He has settled accounts with the whole Jewish doctrine of repentance and reconciliation; he knows how it is only with the *practice* of life that one feels "divine," "blessed," "evangelical," at all times a "child of God."

Not "repentance," not "prayer for the sake of forgiveness" — they are not ways to God; the *evangelical practice alone* leads to God, it precisely *is* "God"! — What was *abolished* with the gospel was the Judaism of the concepts "sin," "forgiveness of sin," "faith," "salvation through faith" — the whole Jewish church teaching was denied in the "glad tidings."

The profound instinct for how one would have to *live* in order to feel "in heaven," in order to feel "eternal," while in every other situation one feels oneself absolutely *not* "in heaven": this alone is the psychological reality of "redemption." — A new way of living, *not* a new faith ...

34

If I understand anything about this great symbolist, it is that he took only *inner* realities as realities, as "truths" — that he understood the rest, everything natural, temporal, spatial, historical only as signs, as opportunities for analogy. The concept "Son of Man" is not a concrete person belonging to history, something individual, unique, but an "eternal" factuality, a psychological symbol released from the concept of time. The same applies once more, and in the highest sense, to the *God* of this typical symbolist, to the "kingdom of God," to the "kingdom of heaven," to "God's having a Son." Nothing is more un-Christian than the *ecclesiastical crudities* of a God as person, of a "kingdom of God which is *to come*, of a "heavenly kingdom" *beyond*, of a "Son of God," the second person of the Trinity. This is all — forgive the expression — like a fist in the eye — oh in what an eye! — of the Gospel: *world-historical cynicism* in the mockery of a symbol... But the answer lies right at hand concerning what is being touched upon with the sign of "Father" and "Son" — not at every hand, I confess: with the word "Son" there is expressed the *entrance* into the total transfigurative feeling of all things (eternal bliss), with the "Father" *this feeling itself*, the feeling of eternity, the feeling of perfection. — I am ashamed to recall what the Church has made of this symbolism: has it not placed an Amphitryon story at the threshold of Christian "faith"? And a dogma of "immaculate conception" over and above it?... *But with that it has maculated conception.* — —

The "kingdom of heaven" is a condition of the heart — not something that comes "over the earth" or "after death." The whole concept of natural death is lacking in the Gospel: death is no bridge, no crossing, it is lacking because it belongs to a completely different, merely apparent, merely useful-as-a-sign world. The "hour of death" is *no* Christian concept — the "hour," the time, physical life and its crises simply do not exist for the teacher of the "glad tidings"... the "kingdom of God "is not at all what one expects; it has no yesterday and no day after tomorrow, it does not come in a "thousand years" — it is an experience of the heart; it is everywhere, it is nowhere...

35

This "bringer of glad tidings" died as he had lived, as he had *taught* — *not* to "save mankind," but to show how one ought to live. It is the *practice* which he bequeathed to mankind: his behavior before the judges, before the bailiffs, before the accusers and all manner of slander and scorn — his behavior on the *cross*. He does not resist, he does not defend his rights, he takes no step to protect himself against the worst that can happen to him, what is more, *he positively demands it* ... And he entreats, he suffers, he loves *with* those, *in* those, who do him evil. His words to the *thief* on the cross contain the whole Gospel. "That was truly a *divine* man, a child of God!" — says the thief. "If you feel this" — answers the Savior — "then you are *in Paradise*, then you are a child of God." *Not* to resist, *not* to get angry, *not* to hold accountable ... And not to oppose even the evil one — to *love* him...

36

— Only we, we *free-gotten* spirits, have the prerequisite for understanding something nineteen centuries have misunderstand — that instinct and passion become integrity which wages war on the "holy lie" even more than on any other lie... They were immeasurably removed from our loving and careful neutrality, from that cultivation of the spirit through which alone the divining of such unfamiliar, such tender things is made possible: they desired at all times, with a shameless selfishness, only *their own* advantage, they erected the *Church* out of opposition to the Gospel...

If one were to look for signs that behind the great world-game an ironical divinity had control at his fingertips, he would find no small support in the *enormous question mark* called Christianity. That mankind is on its knees in opposition to that which was the origin, the meaning, the *right* of the Gospel, that in the concept "Church" it pronounced holy precisely that which the "bringer of glad tidings" felt to be *beneath* him, *behind* him — one searches in vain for a greater form of *world-historical irony* — —

37

— Our age is proud of its historical sense: how could it make believable the nonsense that at the beginning of Christianity there stands the *crude miracle-worker and savior fable* — and that everything spiritual and symbolic is only a later development? On the contrary: the history of Christianity — and that beginning in fact with the death on the cross — is the history of the step by step, ever cruder misunderstanding of an *original* symbolism. With every diffusion of Christianity over still broader, still rawer masses in whom the presuppositions out of which it was born are ever more lacking it became more necessary to *vulgarize*, to *barbarize* Christianity — it has gulped down the doctrines and rites of all the *subterranean* cults of the *imperium Romanum*, gulped down the nonsense of all kinds of sick reason. The fate of Christianity lies in the necessity that its faith had to itself become as sick, as low and vulgar, as the necessities it was meant to satisfy were sick, low, and vulgar. In the character of the Church this *sick barbarism* itself added up to power — the Church, this form of deadly enmity to all integrity, to all *loftiness* of the soul, to all cultivation of the spirit, to all candid and kind humanity. The *Christian* values — the *noble* values: only we, we *free-gotten* spirits, have restored this greatest value-antithesis there is! —

38

— At this point I do not suppress a sigh. There are days when a feeling blacker than the blackest melancholy visits me — the *contempt for man*. And to leave no doubt about *what* I despise, *whom* I despise: it is the man of today, the man with whom I am fatefully contemporary. The man of today — I choke on his unclean breath... Towards the past I have, like all knowledgeable ones, a great tolerance, that is to say, a *magnanimous* self-control: I pass through the madhouse-world of whole millennia, whether it be called "Christianity," "Christian belief," "Christian Church" with a gloomy caution — I take care not to make mankind answerable for its mental disorders. But my feeling changes, breaks out, as soon as I enter the modern age, *our* age. Our age is *aware*... What was formerly just sick has today become indecent — it is indecent to be a Christian today. *And here begins my disgust.* — I look around me: there is not a word left anymore of what was formerly called "truth," we cannot stand it anymore if a priest so much as utters the word "truth." Even with the most modest claim to integrity one *must* know today that a theologian, a priest, a pope, with every sentence he speaks, not only errs, but *lies* — that he is no longer free to lie out of "innocence," out of "ignorance." Also the priest knows, as well as everyone knows, that there is no "God" anymore, no "sins," no "Savior" — that "free will," "moral world-order" are *lies* — seriousness, profound self-overcoming of the spirit no longer *permits* anyone *not* to know about this ... All the concepts of the Church are recognized for what they are, the most *malicious* counterfeiting there is, for the purpose of *devaluing* nature and natural values; the priest himself is recognized for what he is, the most dangerous kind of parasite, the true poison-spider of life ... We know, our *conscience* knows it today — , *what* those sinister inventions of the priest and the Church are generally worth, to what end they have served in attaining that condition of mankind's self-violation, the view of which is enough to make a person sick — the concepts "other world," "Last Judgment," "immortality of the soul," the "soul" itself: they are instruments of torture, they are forms of cruelty by virtue of which the priest became master, remained master... Everybody knows this: *and in spite of this everything remains as before.* Where have the last feelings of decency, of self-respect gone when even our statesmen, an otherwise very unbiased kind of men and anti-Christians in deed through and through, still call themselves Christians today and go to communion? ... A young prince at the head of his regiment, magnificent as the expression of his people's egotism and self-conceit — but *without* any shame in professing himself a Christian! *Whom* then does Christianity deny? *What* does it call "world"? That one is a soldier, that one is a judge, that one is a patriot; that one defends himself; that one stands upon his honor; that one desires his advantage; that one is *proud* ... every practice of every moment, every instinct, every valuation which becomes *deed* is today anti-Christian: What a *monstrosity of falsity* the modern man must be, that in spite of this he is still *not ashamed* to call himself a Christian!

39

— I will go back, I will tell the *true* story of Christianity. — The word "Christianity" is already a misunderstanding — , in reality there has only been one Christian, and he died on the cross. The "Evangel" *died* on the cross. What was called "Evangel" from this moment on was already the opposite of what *he* had lived: "*bad tidings*," a dysangel. It is false to the point of nonsense to see in a "belief," perhaps the belief in salvation through Christ, the mark of distinction of a Christian: only Christian practice, a life such as he who died on the cross *lived*, is Christian ... *Such* a life is possible still today, for *certain* men even necessary: the true, the original Christianity will be possible at all times ... *Not* a believing but a doing, a *not*-doing-much above all, another kind of *being* ... States of consciousness, any kind of belief, a holding-something-for-true for example — every psychologist knows this — are fifth-rate and matters of complete indifference indeed compared to the value of the instincts: speaking more strictly, the whole concept of spiritual causality is false. To reduce being a Christian, Christianness, to a holding-something-for-true, to a mere phenomenalism of consciousness, means to negate Christianness. *In reality there have been no Christians at all.* The "Christian," that which has been called Christian for the last two thousand years, is merely a psychological self-misunderstanding. Looked at more closely, *despite* all belief it is *merely* the instincts which have prevailed in him — and what instincts! — "Belief" has been at all times, for example in Luther; only a cloak, a cover, a *curtain* behind which the instincts played their game — , a clever *blindness* about the dominance of *certain* instincts... "Belief" — I have already called it the true Christian *shrewdness,* — one always spoke of "belief," one always *acted* only out of instinct ... In the Christian world of ideas there is nothing that even touches upon reality: on the other hand, we have recognized in the instinctive hatred *toward* reality the driving force, the only driving force at the root of Christianity. What follows from this? That *in psychologicis* as well the error here is radical, that is, essence-determining, that is, a matter of *substance.* *One* concept removed here, a single reality put in its place — and the whole of Christianity crumbles into nothingness! Viewed from a height, this strangest of all facts, a religion dependent on errors but inventive and even ingenious *only* through destructive, *only* through life- and heart-poisoning errors, remains a *spectacle for the gods* — for those deities who are at the same time philosophers and whom I have encountered, for example, during those famous dialogues on Naxos. The moment *nausea* leaves them (— *and* leaves us!), they are thankful for the Christian spectacle: perhaps only for the sake of *this* curious case that pitiful star called earth deserves a divine glance, a bit of divine interest ... For let us not underrate the Christian: the Christian, false *to the point of innocence,* is far above the ape — with regard to Christians a well-known theory of descent becomes mere politeness.

40

— The fate of the Evangel was decided with his death — it hung on "the cross" ... Only his death, this unexpected, ignominious death, only the cross, which was reserved in general merely for the *canaille* — only this most atrocious paradox brought them face to face with the real riddle: *who was that? what was that?* — The shocked and deeply offended feeling, the suspicion that such a death might be the refutation of their cause, the terrible question mark "why exactly this way?"

— this condition is understood only too well. Here everything *had* to be necessary, *had* to have meaning *had* to make sense, make sense in the highest degree; a disciple's love knows no chance. Only now the cleft split apart: "*who* had him killed? *who* was his natural enemy?" — this question sprang forth like a bolt of lightning. Answer: *ruling* Jewry, its highest class. From this moment one felt oneself in revolt *against* the ruling order, one subsequently understood Jesus as being *in revolt against the ruling order.* Until then this warlike, this nay-saying, this no-doing characteristic was *absent* from his image; even more, he was the antithesis of it. Evidently the little community did *not* understand precisely the main thing, the prefigurative element in this manner of death, the freedom from, the ascendancy *over*, every feeling of *ressenti-ment:* — a sign of how little they understood him after all! Jesus himself could have desired nothing by his death other than to give the strongest test, the *proof* of his doctrine... But his disciples were far from *forgiving* this death — which would have been evangelical in the highest sense; or even *proposing* the same death for themselves in soft and lovely repose of the heart ... Precisely that most unevangelical of feelings, *revenge*, came out on top again. It was impossible that the matter could come to an end with this death: they required "retribution," "judgment" (— and yet what could be more unevangelical than "retribution," "punishment," "sitting in judgment"!). Once again the popular expectation of a Messiah came into the foreground; a historical moment became fixed in our eye: the "kingdom of God" is coming in judgment over its enemies ... But with this everything is misunderstood: the "kingdom of God" as final act, as promise! For the Evangel had clearly been the presence, the fulfillment, the "reality" of this "kingdom." Precisely such a death *was* this very "kingdom of God." Only now was all the contempt and bitterness toward the Pharisees worked into the type of the master — they made a Pharisee and theologian out of him thereby! On the other hand, the reverence run wild of these totally unhinged souls could no longer stand that evangelical right of everyone to be a child of God, which Jesus had taught: their revenge was to exalt Jesus in an excessive way, severing themselves

from him: just as the Jews had formerly, out of revenge on their enemies, separated their God from themselves and raised him on high.
The *one* God and the *one* Son of God: both products of *ressentiment*...

41

— And from then on an absurd problem emerged: "How *could*
God allow this!" Thereupon the disturbed reason of the little community found a just terribly absurd answer: God gave his Son for the forgiveness of sins, as a *sacrifice*. Suddenly it was all over with the Gospel!
The *expiatory sacrifice*, and that in its most loathsome, barbaric form,
the sacrifice of the *innocent one* for the sins of the guilty! What horrible
paganism! — Jesus had certainly abolished the very concept of "guilt"
— he had denied any gap between God and man, he had *lived* this
unity of God and man as *his* "glad tidings" ... And *not* as a prerogative!
— And from then on there entered into the type of the Savior step by
step: the doctrine on judgment and on the Second Coming, the doctrine on death as an expiatory death, the doctrine on the *Resurrection*,
with which the whole concept of "blessedness," the whole and sole
reality of the Evangel, is juggled away — in favor of a condition *after*
death! ... Paul, with that rabbinical insolence which distinguishes him
at all points, logicalized this concept, this *indecency* of a concept, thus:
"*If* Christ is not resurrected from the dead, then our faith is in vain." —
And all at once the Evangel became the most contemptible of all
unfulfillable promises, the most *shameless* doctrine of personal immortality ... Paul even taught it as a *reward*!...

42

One sees *what* was at an end with the death on the Cross: a new, a
completely original start to a Buddhistic peace movement, to an
actual, *not* merely promised, *happiness on earth*. For this is — I have
already called special attention to it — the fundamental difference
between the two *décadence* religions: Buddhism promises nothing but

delivers; Christianity promises everything, but *delivers nothing.* — On the heels of the glad tidings "came the *worst of all*: those of Paul: In Paul was embodied the opposite type to the "bringer of glad tidings," the genius in hatred, in the vision of hatred, in the pitiless logic of hatred. *What* all did this dysangelist bring as a sacrifice to his hatred! Above all else the Savior: he nailed Him to *His* cross. The life, the example, the teaching, the death, the meaning and the right of the whole Gospel — nothing was left over once this counterfeiter on account of hatred had grasped what he alone could make use of. *Not* the reality, not the historical truth ... And once more the priestly instinct of the Jew perpetrated the same great crime against history — Paul simply crossed out the yesterday, the day before yesterday, of Christianity, he *devised for himself a history of early Christianity.* Even more: he falsified the history of Israel once again in order to make it seem the prehistory for *his* deed: all the prophets had spoken of *his* "Savior"... The Church later falsified even the history of mankind into the prehistory of Christianity... The type of the Savior, the doctrine, the practice, the death, the meaning of the death, even the aftermath of the death — nothing remained untouched, nothing remained even close to the reality. Paul simply shifted the emphasis of that whole existence *beyond* this existence — in the *lie* of the "resurrected" Jesus. He really could not use the life of the Savior — he had need of the death on the cross *and* something else besides... To consider honorable a Paul whose home was the main seat of Stoic enlightenment when he arranges for himself from an hallucination the proof of the Savior's *still* being alive, or even to give credence to his story *that* he had this hallucination would be true *niaiserie* on the part of a psychologist: Paul wanted an end, *consequently* he also wanted a means... What he himself did not believe, the idiots among whom he scattered *his* teaching did believe. — His requirement was *power*; with Paul the priest wanted power once more — he could only use concepts, teachings, symbols, by which one tyrannizes masses, forms herds. *What* alone did Mohammed later borrow from Christianity? Paul's invention, his means for priestly tyranny, for herd formation: the belief in immortality — *that is, the teaching on* "judgment"...

43

If one misplaces the emphasis of life by shifting it *not* into life but into the "beyond" — into *nothingness* — , then one has taken from life its emphasis in general. The great lie of personal immortality destroys all reason, all natural instinct — everything that is beneficent, life-promoting, and future-assuring in the instincts arouses mistrust from now on. *So* to live that there is no longer any meaning in life, *that* now becomes the "meaning" of life... To what purpose public spirit, to what purpose descent and ancestors, to what purpose working together, trusting, promoting any sort of general welfare and keeping it in sight? ... Just so many "experiments," just so many diversions from the "right way" — "one thing is necessary"... That everyone as an "immortal soul" has equal rank with everyone else, that in the totality of all living things the "salvation" of *each* individual is allowed to claim eternal significance, that little hypocrites and three-quarters lunatics are allowed to flatter themselves that for their sake the laws of nature are continually being *broken* — such an elevation of every sort of self-ishness into the infinite, into the *impudent*, one cannot brand with enough contempt. And yet Christianity owes *its* victory to *this* wretched flattery before personal vanity — precisely all the misfits, the revolutionary-minded, all those who took the wrong path, the whole refuse and remains of mankind it won over to itself with this. The "salvation of the soul" — in plain English: "The world revolves around *me*"... The poison of the doctrine "*equal* rights for all" — Christianity sowed this seed most fundamentally: from the most secluded nooks and crannies of base instincts Christianity has waged a war to the death against every feeling of reverence and distance between man and man, that which is the prerequisite to every enhancement, every increase in culture — from the *ressentiment* of the masses it has forged its *main weapon* against *us*, against everything noble, joyful, generous on earth, against our happiness on earth... "Immortality" granted to every Peter and Paul has been the greatest, most malevolent attempt hith-erto on the life of *noble* humanity. — *And* let us not underestimate the fatality that has crept out of Christianity and down into politics! No one today has the courage any longer for separate rights, for sovereign rights, for a feeling of reverence for oneself and one's like — for a *pathos of distance* ... Our politics is *sick* from this lack of courage! — The aristocracy of sentiment has been undermined in the most underground way by the lie of the equality of souls: and if belief in the "prerogative of the majority" makes and *will make* revolutions — it is Christianity, no question about it, it is *Christian* value judgments which every revolution simply translates into blood and misdeed! Christianity is a rebellion of all that is crawling on the ground against whatever has *height*: the gospel of the "lowly" *makes* low ...

44

— The gospels are invaluable as testimony to the already irresistible corruption *within* the first community. What Paul later carried to its conclusion with the logical cynicism of a rabbi was nonetheless merely the process of decline which began with the death of the Savior. — One cannot read these gospels carefully enough; there are difficulties behind every word. I confess, assuming one will make allowances for me, that they are just for that reason a first-rate pleasure for a psychologist — as the *opposite* of all naïve depravity, as refinement *par excellence*, as artistry in psychological depravity. The gospels stand alone. The Bible in general bears no comparison. One is among Jews: *first* consideration in order not to lose the thread completely here. The sheer genius here of self-dissembling turning into "holiness," never approached or attained by books or men, this word- and gesture-counterfeiting as an *art*, is not a chance event of some individual talent, some exception of nature. This is due to *race*. In Christianity, holy lying as an art, all of Jewry, a more than century long Jewish preparation and technique of the utmost seriousness, attains its ultimate mastery. The Christian, that *ultimo ratio* of the lie, is the Jew once more — even *thrice* more ... The fundamental will to employ only the concepts, symbols, and attitudes which have been

proved by the practice of priests, the instinctive rejection of every
other practice, every *other* value- and usefulness-perspective — this is
not only tradition, this is *inheritance*: only as inheritance does it function like nature. All of humanity, the best heads of the best times even
(except for one who is perhaps merely a monster —) have let themselves be deceived. The Gospel has been read as a *book of innocence* ... no
small indication of the theatrical mastery displayed here. — Certainly
if we got to *see* them, even if only in passing, all these strange yes-men
and synthetic holy men, then it would be at an end — and it is precisely because I cannot read a word *without* seeing gestures that *I make
an end with them...* They have a certain way of turning up their eyes that I
cannot abide. Luckily, for the great majority books are merely *literature*
— — One must not let oneself be misled: "Judge not!" they say, but
they send to hell everything that stands in their way. In letting God
judge, they themselves judge; in glorifying God, they glorify themselves; in *demanding* just those virtues of which they are capable —
even more, those which they need in order to stay on top generally — ,
they assume the great appearance of struggling for virtue, of fighting
for the sovereignty of virtue. "We live, we die, we sacrifice ourselves
for the good" (— "the truth," "the light," the "kingdom of God"): in
truth, they do what they cannot help doing. Getting themselves to
resemble dissemblers, sitting in a corner, living a shadowy existence
there in the shadows, they make a *duty* out of this: their life of humility
appears to be a duty; as humility it is one more proof of piety ... Ah this
humble, chaste, merciful mode of mendaciousness! "For us virtue itself
shall bear witness"... One should read the gospels as books of seduc-
tion in company with *morality*: morality has an embargo laid on it by
these petty people — they know how important morality is! Humanity is best *led by the nose* with morality! — The reality is that here the
most conscious *arrogance of the elect* plays at being modest: one has
placed *oneself,* the community," the good and just" once and for all on
one side, on the side of "truth" — and the rest "the world," on the
other... *This* was the most fateful sort of megalomania that has yet
existed on earth: little abortions of creeps and liars began to claim for

themselves the concepts of "God," "truth," "light," "spirit," "love," "wisdom," "life," as if they were synonyms for themselves, for fixing themselves limits against the "world," little superlative Jews, ripe for every kind of lunatic asylum, twisted around values in general to suit *themselves,* as if only the "Christian" were the meaning, the salt, the measure, also the *Last Judgment,* of all the rest ... The whole disaster was only rendered possible because there was already a related, racially related, type of megalomania in the world, the *Jewish* type: as soon as the gap opened up between Jews and Jewish Christians, the latter had no choice but to employ *against* the Jews the same procedures for self-preservation which the Jewish instinct advised, whereas till now the Jews had only employed them against all things *non-*Jewish. The Christian is just a Jew of a "freer" persuasion. —

45

— I give a few examples of what these small people have taken into their heads, what they *have put into the mouth* of their master: nothing but confessions of "beautiful souls." —

"And whosoever shall not receive you, nor hear you, when ye depart thence, shake off the dust under your feet for a testimony against them. Verily I say unto you, It shall be more tolerable for Sodom and Gomorrah in the day of judgment, than for that city."(Mark 6:11). — How *evangelic!*

"And whosoever shall offend one of these little ones that believe in me, it is better for him that a millstone were hanged about his neck, and he were cast into the sea." (Mark 9:42). — How *evangelic!* ...

"And if thine eye offend thee, pluck it out: it is better for thee to enter into the kingdom of God with one eye, than having two eyes to be cast into hell fire: Where their worm dieth not, and the fire is not quenched." (Mark 9:47). — It is not exactly the eye that is meant ...

"Verily I say unto you, That there be some of them that stand here, which shall not taste of death, till they have seen the kingdom of God come with power." (Mark 9:1) — Well *lied,* lion ...

"Whosoever will come after me, let him deny himself, and take up his cross, and follow me. *For ... (Observation of a psychologist)*. Christian morality is refuted by its "*fors*": its "reasons" refute — thus is it Christian.) Mark 8:34. —

"Judge not, *that* ye be not judged. For with what judgment ye judge, *ye* shall be judged. (Matthew 7:1). — What a concept of justice, from a "just" judge! ...

"For if ye love them which love you, *what reward have ye*? do not even the publicans the same? And if ye salute your brethren only, *what do ye more than others*? do not even the publicans so?" (Matthew 5:46) — Principle of "Christian love": in the end it wants to be well-*paid* ...

"But if *ye* forgive not men their trespasses, neither will your Father forgive your trespasses." (Matthew 6:15). — Very compromising for said "Father"...

"But seek ye first the kingdom of God, and his righteousness; and all these things shall be added unto you." (Matthew 6:33). All these things: namely, food, clothing, all the necessities of life. An *error*, to put it mildly... Shortly before that God appears as a tailor, at least in certain cases...

"Rejoice ye in that day and leap for joy: *for*, behold, your reward is great in heaven: for in the like manner did their fathers unto the prophets." (Luke 6:23). — *Impertinent* rabble! They dare to compare themselves to the prophets ...

"Know ye not that ye are the temple of God, and that the Spirit of God dwelleth in you? If any man defile the temple of God, *him shall God destroy*; for the temple of God is holy, *which temple ye are*." (Paul I Cor. 3:16) — this sort of thing one cannot despise enough ...

"Do ye not know that the saints shall judge the world? And if the world shall be judged by *you*, are ye unworthy to judge the smallest matters?" (Paul I Cor. 6:2) Unfortunately not merely the speech of a madhouse inhabitant ... This *frightful swindler* goes on literally: "Know ye not that *we* shall judge angels? How much more things that pertain to this life?" ...

"Hath not God made foolish the wisdom of this world? For after that in the wisdom of God the world by wisdom knew not God, it pleased God by the foolishness of preaching to save them that believe... ; not many wise men after the flesh, not many mighty, not many noble are called: But *God hath chosen the foolish things of the world* to confound the wise; and God hath chosen the weak things of the world to confound the things which are mighty; And base things of the world, and things which are despised, hath God chosen, yea, and things which are not, to bring to naught things that are: That no flesh should glory in his presence.' (Paul I Cor. 1:20 ff.). — To *understand* this passage, one should read the first essay of my *Genealogy of Morals:* in it there was first set forth the contrast between a noble morality and a chandala morality, one born out of *ressentiment* and impotent vengeful-ness. Paul was the greatest of all apostles of vengefulness...

46

— *What follows from this?* That one does well to put on gloves when reading the New Testament. The nearness of so much uncleanliness almost forces one to do so. We would as little choose to associate with the "first Christians" as we would with Polish Jews: not that a single pretext would be needed against them: both of them do not smell good. — I have searched in vain in the New Testament to spy out even one sympathetic feature; there is nothing in it which is free, kindly, candid, honest. Humanity has not yet taken its first step here — the instincts of cleanliness are lacking... There are only *bad* instincts in the New Testament, there is not even any courage for these bad instincts. Everything in it is cowardice, everything is closing one's eyes and self – deceiving. Every book becomes clean when one has just read the New Testament; to give an example, immediately after reading Paul I read with delight that most graceful, most playful scoffer Petronius, of whom one could say what Domenico Boccaccio wrote to the Duke of Parma concerning Cesare Borgia: "è tutto festo" — immortally healthy, immortally cheerful and successful... For these little creeps miscalculate in the main thing. They attack, but everything they attack is *distinguished* thereby. He whom a "first Christians" attacks is *not* besmirched by him... On the contrary: it is an honor to have "first Christians" against one. One does not read the New Testament without having a preference for those who are mishandled therein, — not to mention the "wisdom of this world," which an insolent braggart "through foolish preaching" seeks in vain to put to shame... But even the Scribes and Pharisees receive an advantage from having such opponents: they must have indeed been worth something to be hated in such an indecent way. Hypocrisy — what a reproach for the "first Christians" *to dare* to make! — In the end it was that the Scribes and Pharisees were the *privileged:* this sufficed, chandala hatred requires no further reasons. The "first Christian" — I fear, also the "last Christian," *whom I may perhaps yet live to see* — is in his lowest instincts a rebel against everything privileged — he lives, he fights continually for "equal rights"... Looked at more closely, he has no choice. If in his person he wants to be a "chosen of God" — or a "temple of God:, or a "judge of angels" — , then every *other* principle of choice, by integrity for example, by spirit, by manliness and pride, by beauty and liberty of the heart, is simply "world" — *evil as such*... Moral: every word in the mouth of a "first Christian" is a lie, every action he performs an instinctive falsehood — all his values, all his goals are unhealthy, but *whomever* he hates, *whatever* he hates, *that has value*... The Christian, the priestly Christian especially, is a *criterion of values* — — Do I need to add that in the whole New Testament there appears but one *single* figure who commands respect? Pilate, the Roman governor. To take a Jewish affair *seriously* — he could not persuade himself to that. One Jew more or less — what does it matter? ... The noble scorn of a Roman before whom a shameless misuse of the word "truth" was exercised has enriched the New Testament with the only expression *that has value* — that is its critique, its *destruction* even: "What is truth?"...

47

— This does not set *us* apart, that we find no God again, neither in history, nor in nature, nor behind nature — but that we feel what has been revered as God to be not "godly" but pitiful, absurd, harmful, not merely an error but a *crime against life*... We deny God as God... If one were to prove this God of the Christians to us, we would know still less how to believe in him. — In a formula: *deus, qualem Paulus creavit, dei negatio.* (The God which Paul created is the negation of God:) — A religion like Christianity, which has no point of contact with reality, which falls away immediately as soon as reality achieves validity at even one point, must naturally be a deadly enemy to the "wisdom of the world," meaning *science* — it will approve of all means by which the cultivation of the intellect, that purity and severity of intellectual matters of conscience, the noble coolness and freedom of the intellect, can be poisoned, slandered, *condemned.* "Faith" as an imperative is the *veto* against science — *in praxi*, the lie at any price... Paul *perceived* that the lie — that faith was necessary: the Church in return later perceived Paul. — That "God" which Paul invented for himself, the one who "confounds the wisdom of the world" (in a narrower sense the two great opponents of all superstition, philology and medicine), is in truth only the resolute *determination* of Paul himself to do this: to call his own will "God," *Torah*, that is Jewish to the core. Paul *wants* to confound "the wisdom of the world": his enemies are the *good* philologists and physicians of Alexandrian schooling — , he wages war against them. Indeed, one is not a philologist or a physician without also being at the same time an anti-Christian. For as a philologist one sees *behind* the "holy books," as a physician one sees *behind* the physiological depravity of the typical Christian. The physician says "incurable," the philologist "swindle"...

48

— Has anyone actually understood the famous story that stands at the beginning of the Bible — of God's hellish terror in the presence of *science?*... No one has understood it. This priestly book *par excellence* begins, as expected, with the great inner difficulty of the priest: *he* has only *one* great danger, *consequently* "God" has only *one* great danger. — The old God, all "spirit," all high priest, all perfection, takes a pleasure stroll in his garden: except that he is bored. Against boredom the gods themselves fight in vain. What does he do? He invents man — man is entertaining... But, lo and behold, man too is bored. God's sympathy with the only kind of distress possessed by every paradise knows no bounds: he creates still other animals forthwith. God's *first* mistake: man did not find the animals entertaining — he dominated over them, he did not even want to be an "animal." — Consequently God created woman. And indeed there was now an end to boredom — but to something else as well! Woman was God's *second* mistake. — "Woman is by her nature serpent, Heva" — every priest knows that; "*every* evil comes into the world through woman" — *every priest knows that as well.* *Consequently science* comes through her also. Only through woman did man learn to taste of the tree of knowledge. — What had happened? The old God was seized with hellish terror. Man himself had become His *greatest* mistake, God had created for himself a rival; science makes one *like God,* — it is all over with priests and gods once man becomes scientific! — Moral: science is the forbidden-in-itself — it alone is forbidden. Science is the *first* sin, the germ of all sins, the *original* sin. *This alone is morality* — "Thou shalt *not* know." — the rest follows from this. — The hellish terror of God did not hinder him from being clever. How can one *protect* oneself against science? For a long time that was his main problem. Answer: away with man out of his paradise! Happiness, idleness give rise to thoughts — all thoughts are bad thoughts ... Man *shalt* not think. — and the priest-in-himself invents distress, death, pregnancy at the risk of one's life, every kind of misery, old age, affliction, above all *sickness* — nothing but means in the fight with science! Distress does not *allow* man to think... And nevertheless! horrible! The structure of knowledge towers up, heavens-storming, gods-twilighting — what to do! — The old God comes up with *war*, he divides the peoples, he makes men mutually destroy one another (— the priests have always found war necessary ...). War — among other things a great mischief-maker with science! — Unbelievable! Knowledge, *emancipation from the priest*, increases in spite of wars. And a final resolution comes to the old God: "Man has become scientific — *it cannot be helped, he must be drowned!*"...

49

— I have been understood. The beginning of the Bible contains the *entire* psychology of the priest. — The priest knows only *one* great danger: that is science — the healthy concept of cause and effect. But upon the whole science flourishes only under happy circumstances — one must have time, one must have spirit *to spare*, in order to "know"... "*Consequently* we must make man unhappy" — this was at all times the logic of the priest. — One can already guess *what* first came into the world thereby in accordance with this logic — "sin" ... The concept of guilt and punishment, the entire "moral-world-order" was invented *contrary to* science — *contrary to* man's emancipation from the priest ... Man shall *not* look out from himself, he shall look into himself; he shall *not* look cleverly and carefully into things, as a learner would; he shall not look at all; he shall *suffer* ... And he shall suffer so that he needs the priest at all times. — Away with the physicians! *A Savior is needed.* — The concept of guilt and punishment, including the doctrine on "grace," on "redemption," on "forgiveness" — *lies* through and through and without any psychological reality — were invented in order to destroy man's *causal sense*: they are an assassination attempt against the concept of cause and effect! — and *not* an attempt with fist, with knife, with honesty in hatred and love! But out of the lowest, cunningest, cowardliest instincts! A *priestly* attempt! A *parasite's* attempt! A vampirism of pale subterranean bloodsuckers! ... When the natural results of a deed are no longer "natural," but thought to be caused by the concept-ghosts of superstition, by "God," by "spirits," by "souls" as merely "moral" consequences, as reward, penalty, a sign of affirmation, an aid to education, then the precondition for knowledge is destroyed — then *the greatest crime against humanity has been committed.* — Sin, to say it once more, this form of human self-desecration *par excellence*, was invented in order to make science, culture, every elevation and distinction of mankind impossible; the priest *rules* through the invention of sin. —

50

— I do not absolve myself at this point from presenting a psychology of "belief," of "believers," for the benefit, as is proper, of precisely the "believers." If today there is still no lack of those who do not know in what respect it is unbecoming to be "a believer" — *or* a sign of *décadence*, of a broken will to live — , by tomorrow they will know it. My voice reaches even the hard-of-hearing. — It appears, if I have not misheard otherwise, that among Christians there is a kind of criterion of truth called "proof of strength." "Belief makes blessed: *therefore* it is true." — One might object here first of all that it is precisely the making-blessed which is not proved but only *promised*: blessedness tied to the condition of "belief" — one shall become blessed *because* one believes ... But to actually enter *that* which the priest promises as being a "beyond" inaccessible to any control, how to prove *that*? — The alleged "proof of strength" is therefore at bottom only a belief again that the effect promised by that belief will not fail to appear. In a formula: "I believe that belief makes blessed — *consequently* it is true." — But with this we are already at the end. This "consequently" would be the *absurdum* itself as a criterion of truth. Let us suppose however, with some indulgence, that this making blessed through belief could be proved (*not* only wished for, *not* only promised by the somewhat suspect mouth of a priest): would blessedness — technically speaking, *pleasure* — ever be a proof of truth? So little that it nearly furnishes the counterproof, in any case the highest suspicion against "truth," when feelings of pleasure enter into the discussion on the question "What is true?" The proof by "pleasure" is a proof *of* "pleasure" — nothing more; where in all the world was it established that *true* judgments should give more pleasure than false ones and, in accordance with a pre-established harmony, necessarily bring along pleasant feelings in their train? — The experience of all severe, all profoundly disposed intellects teaches *the reverse*. Truth has had to be fought for every step of the way, almost everything on which the heart otherwise clings, our love, our trust in life, has had to be surrendered for it: the service of the truth is the hardest service. — What does it mean then to be *honest* in intellectual matters? That one is strict towards one's heart, that one despises "beautiful feelings," that one makes every yes and no a matter of conscience! — — — Belief makes blessed: *consequently* it lies ...

51

That under certain circumstances belief makes blessed, that blessedness still does not make a fixed idea into a *true* idea, that faith moves no mountains but I dare say *places* mountains where there are none: a fleeting walk through a *madhouse* clears this up sufficiently. Certainly *not* a priest: for he denies that sickness is sickness, madhouse is madhouse. Christianity *needs* sickness, just as Hellenism needs a surplus of health — making *sick* is the true hidden intention behind the Church's entire salvation procedure system. And the Church itself — is it not the Catholic madhouse as ultimate ideal? — The religious man, as the Church *wants* him, is a typical *décadent*; the moment when a religious crisis gains power over a people is always characterized by epidemics of the nerves; the "inner world" of the religious man is so like the "inner world" of the overstrained and exhausted as to be mistaken for it; the "highest" conditions which Christianity has hung up over mankind as the value of all values are epileptoid forms — only madmen *or* great impostors has the Church canonized in *majorem dei honorem* ... I once allowed myself to express the entire Christian repentance- *and* redemption-*training* as a methodically produced *folie circulaire* (best studied in England today) on, as stands to reason, a soil already prepared beforehand for it, namely, a fundamentally morbid one. No one is free to become a Christian: One does not become "converted" to Christianity — one must be sick enough for it ... We others, we who have *courage* for sound health *and* also for contempt, how *we* ought to have contempt for a religion which teaches misunderstanding of the body! which refuses to get rid of the soul-superstition! Which makes "just deserts" out of an insufficient diet! which combats sound health as a kind of enemy, devil, temptation! which has persuaded itself that one can carry around a "perfect soul" in a cadaver of a body and therefore found it necessary to arrange for itself a new concept of "perfection," a pale, sickly, idiotic-enthusiastic disposition, so-called "holiness" — holiness, itself simply a set of symptoms of the impoverished, enervated, incurably corrupted body! ... The Christian movement, as a European movement, is from the start a collective movement of the outcast- and reject-elements of every kind (— these want to gain power along with Christianity). It does *not* express the decline of a race, it is an aggregate formation of *décadence* forms from everywhere seeking each other out and crowding together. It is *not*, as is generally assumed, the corruption of antiquity itself, of *noble* antiquity, which made possible Christianity: the learned idiocy which even today still maintains such things cannot be opposed harshly enough. At the very time when the sickly, rotten chandala classes in the entire *imperium* were becoming Christian, the *opposite type*, the nobility, was present in its finest and ripest form. The great number became master; the democratism of the Christian instincts *triumphed* ... Christianity has the *rancune* of the sick as its basis, the instinct directed *against* the healthy, *against* good health. Everything well-developed, proud, high-spirited, beauty above all, hurts it in eyes and ears. Once again I recall the invaluable saying from Paul: "The *weak* things of the world, the *foolish* things of the world, the *base* things and the *despised* things of the world hath God chosen": that was the formula, *in hoc signo décadence triumphed. God on the cross* — does anyone still not understand the frightful hidden-thinking behind this symbol? — All that suffers, all that hangs on the cross, is *divine* ... We all hang on the cross, therefore *we* are divine ... We alone are divine ... Christianity was a victory, a *nobler* sentiment perished on account of it — Christianity has thus far been mankind's greatest misfortune. — —

52

Christianity also stands in opposition to all *intellectual* successfulness — it *can* only use sick reasoning as Christian reasoning, it takes the side of everything idiotic, it utters a curse against the "intellect," against the *superbia* of the healthy intellect. Because sickness belongs to the essence of Christianity, the typical Christian condition, "faith," *must* also be a form of sickness, while all straight, honest, scientific paths to knowledge must be repudiated by the Church as *forbidden* paths. Doubt is already a sin... The complete want of psychological cleanliness among priests — given away in a glance — is a *consequential* appearance of *décadence* — observe hysterical females on the one hand, rickets-laden children on the other, to see how regularly instinctive falsehood, lying for the sake of lying, the incapacity for straight glances and steps, is the expression of *décadence*. "Faith" means not-*wanting*-to-know what is true. The pietist, the priest of both sexes, is *false* because he is sick: his instinct *demands* that truth get no chance to shine at any point. "What makes sick is *good*; what comes out of fullness, out of abundance, out of power is *evil*": thus the believers feel. *In bondage to the lie:* that is how I divine every predestined theologian. — Another mark of a theologian is his *inability for philology*. Philology is meant to be understood here, in a general sense, as the art of reading well — to be able to pick up facts *without* falsifying them through interpretation, *without* losing prudence, patience, and elegance in the desire for understanding. Philology as *ephexis* in interpretation: whether it be a question of books, newspaper reports, fate or weather data — not to mention "salvation of the soul" ... The way in which a theologian, no matter whether in Berlin or in Rome, interprets a "passage from Scripture" or an experience, a triumph of arms for the fatherland for example, in the higher light of the Psalms of David, is always so *audacious* that it drives a philologist up the wall. And what is he even to begin to do when pietists and other cows from Swabia dress up the wretched everyday and chamber smoke of their existence, with the "hand of God," into a miracle of "grace," of "providence," of "salvation experiences"! The most modest expenditure of intelligence, not to mention decency, ought to bring these interpreters to where they convince themselves of the complete childishness and unworthiness of such an abuse of divine dexterity. Even with so small an amount of piety in our body, we ought to find a God who cures a head cold at the right time or allows us to climb into a coach just at the moment when a cloudburst commences such an absurd God that he would have to be abolished even if he existed. A God as servant, as postman, as almanac consultant — at bottom a word for all the stupidest sort of accidents ... "Divine providence," as it is still believed in today by approximately every third man in "cultured Germany" would be an objection to God stronger than any that could possibly be imagined. And in any case it is an objection to the Germans! ...

53

— That *martyrs* prove anything about a cause is so far from being true that I would deny a martyr has ever had anything to do with the truth. The tone with which a martyr throws his deeming-as-true into the face of society already expresses such a low level of intellectual integrity, such *obtuseness* to the question of "truth" that one never needs to refute a martyr. Truth is not something one person might have and another not have: peasants at best or peasant-apostles like Luther can think about truth in this fashion. One may be certain that modesty, *moderation*, in this respect, increases according to the degree of conscientiousness in intellectual matters. To *know* five things, and with a gentle hand, decline to know anything *else* ... "Truth," as every prophet, every sectarian, every free spirit, every socialist, every churchman understands the term, is consummate proof that not even a beginning has been made toward that cultivation of the intellect and self-overcoming necessary to find some small, ever so small, truth. — Martyrdoms, by the way, have been a great misfortune in history: they have *misled* ... The inference of all idiots, women and folk included, that a cause for which someone goes to his death (or which even engenders death-seeking epidemics, like the earliest Christianity) must be something of consequence — this inference has become an unspeakable hindrance to examination, to the spirit of caution and examination., Martyrs have *harmed* truth ... Even today it requires only the crudity of a persecution to allow an otherwise indifferent sect to make an *honorable* name for itself. — What? Does it change the value of a cause that someone gave up his life for it? — An error that becomes honorable is an error that possesses one more seductive charm: do you think, you theologian masters, that we would give you an occasion to become martyrs for your lies? One refutes a thing by laying it respectfully on ice — in this way too one refutes theologians ... The world-historical stupidity of all persecutors lay precisely in this, that they gave the opposing cause the appearance of being honorable — that they gave it the fascination of martyrdom as a gift ... Woman today is still on her knees before an error because she has been told that someone died on the cross for it. *Is the cross then an argument?* — — But about all these things one man alone has spoken the word which has been needed for thousands of years — *Zarathustra.*

Signs of blood they wrote on the path that they took, and their folly taught that truth is proved by blood.

But blood is the worst witness of truth; blood poisons even the purest teaching and turns it into delusion and hatred of the heart.

And if someone goes through fire for his teaching — what does that prove? Verily, it means more when out of your own fire your own teaching comes.

54

One should not let oneself be misled: great spirits are skeptics. Zarathustra is a skeptic. Strength, *freedom* on account of the power and superpower of the mind, *proves* itself through skepticism. Men of conviction do not come into consideration at all when it is a question of all things fundamental in value and disvalue. Convictions are prisons. They do not see far enough with them, they do not see *beneath* themselves: but in order to be allowed to participate in the conversation on value and disvalue, one must see five hundred convictions *beneath* oneself — *behind* oneself ... A spirit which wills great things, which wills the means to them as well, is of necessity a skeptic. The freedom from every kind of conviction *pertains*, the *ability* to see things with an open mind... The grand passion, the power and foundation of his being, even more enlightened, even more despotic, than he himself is, takes his whole intellect into service; it makes him unhesitating; it gives him courage even for unholy means; under certain circumstances it *grants* him convictions. Conviction as a *means*: many a thing is achieved only by means of a conviction. Grand passion uses, uses up convictions, it does not submit to them — it knows itself to be sovereign. — Conversely: the need for belief, for some kind of unconditional yes and no, Carlylism, if one will pardon the expression, is a need born out of *weakness*. The man of faith, the "believer" of any sort, is necessarily a dependent man — one who cannot posit *himself* as an end, one who cannot posit any ends at all by himself. The "believer" does not belong to *himself*, he can only be a means, he has to be *used*, he needs someone to use him up. His instinct accords a morality of self-abnegation the highest honor: everything persuades him to it, his intelligence, his experience, his vanity. Every kind of belief is itself an expression of self-abnegation, of self-alienation ... If one considers how necessary the vast majority find a regulation that binds them from without and makes them secure, how the constraint, in a higher sense the *slavery*, is the sole and final condition under which the weaker-willed person, woman especially, can prosper: then one also understands the conviction, the "belief." The man of conviction has his backbone in it. *Not* to see many things, not to be impartial in any respect, to be party through and through to have a strict and necessary perspective with regard to all values — this alone conditions such a kind of man's very existence. But with this he is the antithesis, the *antagonist* of the truthful one — of the truth … The believer is not free to have a conscience at all when it comes to the question of "true" and "untrue": to be upright on this *point* would mean his downfall at once. The pathological conditionality of his perspective makes the convinced man a fanatic — Savonarola, Luther, Rousseau, Robespierre, Saint-Simon — , the antithetical type to the robust spirit, the spirit that has become *free*. But the grand attitude of these *sick* spirits, these concept epileptics, works on the great masses — the fanatics are picturesque, mankind would rather see gestures than hear *reasons* …

55

— A step further in the psychology of conviction, of "belief." It was left for me to ponder a long time ago whether convictions are not more dangerous enemies of truth than lies (Human, All-Too-Human I, Aphorisms 54 and 483). This time I would like to pose the decisive question: is there any difference at all between a lie and a conviction? — All the world believes there is; but what does all the world not believe! Every conviction has its history, its preliminary forms, its trials and errors: it *becomes* conviction, after a long time of *not* existing, after a still longer time of *hardly* existing. What? Could the lie not also be among these embryonic forms of conviction? — Now and then it requires a change in persons: in the son that becomes conviction what in the father was still lie. — I call a lie: *not* wanting to see something that one sees, not wanting to see something *as* one sees it: whether the lie takes place before witnesses or without witnesses does not come into consideration. The most common lie is the one with which a person deceives himself: lying to others is relatively the exception. — Now this *not* wanting to see what one sees, this not wanting to see *as* one sees it, is almost the prime condition for all who are *party* in some sense: the party man becomes of necessity a liar. German historiography, for instance, is convinced that Rome represented despotism, that the Germanic tribes brought the spirit of freedom into the world; what difference is there between this conviction and a lie? Can one still be surprised over it when all parties, German historians as well, instinctively have the big words of morality on their tongues — that morality more or less *continues to exist* because the party man of every sort needs it every moment? "This is *our* conviction: we confess it before all the world, we live and die for it — Respect for all that have convictions!" — I have heard the like even out of the mouths of anti-Semites. On the contrary, gentlemen! An anti-Semite by no means becomes more respectable because he lies out of principle ... The priests, who are sharper in such things and understand very well the objection which lies in the concept of conviction, that is, mendacity as a principle *because* it is purposeful, have here taken over from the Jews the shrewdness to introduce at this point the concept "God," "will of God," "revelation of God." Kant, too, with his categorical imperative, was on the same path: his reason became *practical* in this matter. — There are questions about truth and untruth which are *not* suitable for man to decide; all the highest questions, all the highest problems of value, are beyond human reason ... To grasp the limits of reason — only *that* is true philosophy ... Why did God give man revelation? Would God have done something superfluous? Man is not *capable* of knowing good and evil by himself, therefore God taught him His will ... Moral: the priest does *not* lie — the question of "true" or "untrue" does not *exist* in those things of which the priest speaks; these things do not permit any lying at all. For in order to lie, one must be able to decide *what* is true here. But that is just what man is not *able* to do; the priest is thus only the mouthpiece of God. — Such a priestly syllogism is by no means merely Jewish and Christian; the right to lie and the *shrewdness* belong to the priestly type, to the priests of *décadence* as well as the priests of paganism (— Pagans are all those who say Yes to life, to whom "God" is the expression of the great Yes to all things). — The

"Law," the "will of God," the "Holy Book," "inspiration" — all merely words for the conditions *under* which the priest comes into power, *by* which he maintains his power — these concepts are to be found at the base of all priestly organizations, all priestly or philosophico-priestly power structures. The "holy lie" — common to Confucius, the law-book of Manu, Mohammed, the Christian Church — : it is not absent in Plato. "The truth exists": this means, wherever it is made known, *the priest is lying...*

56

— Ultimately it comes down to what *end* the lie is being told. That in Christianity the "holy" end is absent is *my* objection to its means. Only *bad* ends: poisoning, slandering, the denying of life, the despising of the body, the degrading and self-disfiguring of man through the concept of sin — *consequently* its means are also bad. — I read with an opposite feeling the law-book of Manu, an incomparably spiritual and superior work which even to *mention* in the same breath with the Bible would be a sin against the *spirit*. One guesses immediately: it has an actual philosophy behind it, *in* it, not merely a bad-smelling Judaine of rabbinism and superstition — it gives even the most spoiled psychologist something to chew on. *Not* to forget the main thing, *the* fundamental difference from any sort of Bible: with Manu the *noble* classes, the philosophers and the warriors, have the upper hand over the masses; noble values everywhere, a feeling of perfection, a yea-saying to life, a triumphant sense of well-being towards oneself and towards life — the *sun* shines on the entire book. All the things upon which Christianity vents its unfathomable vulgarity, pro-creation for example, woman, marriage, are here treated seriously, with reverence, with love and confidence. How can one actually put into the hands of women and children a book which contains that vile saying: "To avoid fornication let every man have his own wife, and let every woman have her own husband ... for it is better to marry than to burn"? And how *can* one be a Christian as long as the origin of man is

Christianized, that is *besmirched*, with the concept of the concept of the *immaculate conception?* ... I know of no book in which so many tender and gracious things are said to woman as in the law-book of Manu; these old graybeards and holy men have a way of being well-behaved toward women that has perhaps never been surpassed. "The mouth of a woman" — it says at one point — , "the bosom of a maiden, the prayer of a child, the smoke of an offering are always pure." In another passage: "there is absolutely nothing more pure than the light of the sun, the shadow of a cow, air, water, fire, and the breath of a maiden." A final passage — perhaps also a holy lie — : "All openings of the body above the navel are pure, all openings below impure. Only in the case of a maiden is the whole body pure."

57

One catches the *unholiness* of the Christian aim *in flagranti* once one compares the *Christian* objective with the objective of the Manu law-book — once one throws a bright light on this greatest contrast in objectives. The critic of Christianity is not spared the task of making Christianity *contemptible*. — Such a law-book as that of Manu originates like every good law-book: it summarizes the experience, prudence, and experimental morality of many centuries; it closes down, it produces nothing more. The presupposition for a codification of this sort is the insight that the means of producing a slow and expensively acquired authority for a *truth* are fundamentally different from those by which one would prove it. A law-book never explains the use, the reasons, the casuistry in the previous history of the law: otherwise it would lose the imperative tone, the "thou shalt" which is the presupposition for being obeyed. Herein exactly lies the problem. — At a certain point in the development of a people the most intelligent, that is, the most backward- and forward-seeing class of the same, declare the experience by which one should live — that means *can* live — , to be closed. Their goal is to bring home the richest and fullest harvest possible from the times of experiment and *bad* experience. Consequently, what now must be prevented above all is still further experimentation, the continuation of the fluid state of values, the testing, choosing, criticizing of values *in infinitum*. Against that a double wall is put up: first of all, revelation, which is the assertion that the reason in these laws is *not* of human origin, *not* sought and found slowly and amidst blunders, but coming by way of divine origin, whole, complete, without a history, a present, a miracle, merely communicated ... Then *tradition*, this is the assertion that the law has stood since age-old times, that it would be impious, a crime against one's ancestors, to call it into question. The authority of the law is founded on the thesis ; God *gave* it, our ancestors *lived* it. — The higher rationale in such a procedure lies in the intention to drive consciousness back step by step from what has been recognized as the correct way of life (that is, one *proven* through enormous and sharply-sifted experience): so that a perfect automatism of instinct can be attained — that pre-condition for every kind of mastery, for every kind of perfection in the art of living. To set up a law-book in the manner of Manu means a people is dutybound henceforth to become master, to become perfect — to have ambition for the highest art of life. *Therefore it must be made unconscious:* this is the aim of every holy lie. — The *order of castes*, the supreme, the dominating law, is only the sanctioning of a natural order, natural lawfulness of the first rank, over which no whim, no "modern idea" has power. In every healthy society there are three physiologically differing gravitational types, separated from each other and stipulating mutual opposition to each other, each having its own hygiene, its own work domain, its own kind of mastery and feeling of perfection. Nature, *not* Manu, separates from each other the predominantly spiritual ones, the ones of strong musculature and temperament, and the third type distinguished neither in the one nor in the other, the mediocre ones — the last as the great majority, the first as the elite. The highest caste — I call it *the fewest* — also possesses as the perfect caste the privileges of the fewest: amongst them the displaying of beauty, happiness, and goodness on earth. Only the most spiritual men have allowance to beauty, *to* the beautiful: only with them is kindness not weakness, *Pulchrum est paucorum hominum:* the good is a privilege. On the other hand, nothing suits them less than ugly manners or a pessimistic outlook, an eye that *uglifies* — , or even indignation over the collective aspect of things. Indignation is the privilege of the chandala; pessimism likewise. "The world is perfect" — thus speaks the instinct of the most spiritual, the yea-saying instinct — : "imperfection, every kind of *beneath*-us, distance, the pathos of distance, even the chandala are still part of this kind of perfection." The most spiritual men, as the *strongest,* find their happiness where others would find their downfall: in the labyrinth, in hardness towards oneself and others, in experiment; their delight lies in self-mastery: asceticism is with them nature, need, instinct. The difficult task they consider a privilege; to play with burdens that crush others, a recreation... Knowledge — a form of asceticism. — They are the most venerable kind of man: that does not exclude their being the cheerfullest, the kindliest. They rule not because they want to but because they *are;* they are not free to be second. — The *second* type: they are the guardians of the law, the keepers of order and security; they are the noble warriors, with the *king* above all as the highest formula of warrior, judge, and upholder of the law. The second type are the executives for the most spiritual ones, what is nearest to them, what belongs to them, what removes for them everything *coarse* in the work of ruling — their retinue, their right hand, their best pupils. — In all this, to say it once again, there is nothing capricious, nothing "manufactured"; whatever is different is manufactured — nature is then foiled ... The order of castes, the *order of rank,* formulates only the highest law of life itself; the separation of the three types is necessary for the preservation of society, for making possible the higher and highest types — the *inequality* of rights is the first condition for the existence of any rights at all. — A right is a privilege. In his way of being each person has his own privilege as well. Let us not underrate the privileges of the *mediocre.* Life gets harder and harder according to the *height* — the coldness increases, the accountability increases. A high culture is a pyramid: it can stand only on a broad base, it has first of all a strong and soundly consolidated mediocrity as a prerequisite. Handicraft, trade, agriculture, *science*, the greater part of art, in a word the whole substance of *professional* activity, is thoroughly consistent only with a mediocrity in desire and ability; these things would be out of place among the elite, the instinct pertaining to them opposed to aristocracy as well as anarchism. To be of public use, a wheel, a function, for this there is a natural vocation: it is *not* society but the *kind* of happiness of which the vast majority are alone capable that makes of them intelligent machines. For the mediocre, to be mediocre is a form of happiness; mastery in one thing; a specialty, is a natural instinct. It would be completely unworthy of a deeper mind to find an objection in mediocrity as such. It is even the *foremost* requirement for there being exceptions: a high culture depends on it. When the exceptional man handles precisely the mediocre more tenderly than he does himself or his equals, this is not mere politeness of the heart — it is simply his *duty* ... Whom do I hate most among the rabble of today? The socialist rabble, the chandala apostles who undermine the worker's instinct, pleasure, and feeling of satisfaction with his small existence — who make him envious, who teach him vengefulness... Injustice never lies in unequal rights; it lies in the demand for "equal" rights... What is *bad*? But I have said it already: everything that stems from weakness, from envy, from *vengefulness*. — The anarchist and the Christian have a common origin...

58

Indeed it does make a difference to what end one lies: Whether one preserves thereby or *destroys*. One may set up a complete equation between *Christian* and *anarchist*: their end, their instinct tends only towards destruction. One only has to read history for the proof of this proposition: it is contained there in terrible clarity. If we have just now become acquainted with a religious legislation whose aim it was to "eternalize" the highest condition for the *prospering* of life, a great organization of society — Christianity found its mission in putting an end to just such a society *because in it life prospered*. There the proceeds of reason from long ages of experimentation and uncertainty were to be invested for the most distant use, and a harvest as great, as rich, as complete as possible was to be brought home: here, on the contrary, the harvest was *poisoned* overnight... That which stood *aere perennius*, the *imperium Romanum*, the most magnificent form of organization under difficult conditions which has hitherto been achieved, in comparison with which everything before, everything since, is patchwork, bungling, dilettantism — these holy anarchists made it an act of "piety" to destroy "the world," that is, the *imperium Romanum*, until no stone was left unturned — until even Teutons and other louts could be master over it... The Christian and the anarchist: both *décadents*, both incapable of doing anything but dissolving, poisoning, depriving, *bloodsucking*, both with an instinct of *deadly hatred* toward everything that stands, that stands there great, that has duration, that promises life a future... Christianity was the vampire of the *imperium Romanum* — the tremendous deed of the Romans to gain the soil for a great culture *which has time* was undone overnight by it. — Do you still not understand it? The *imperium Romanum* which we know, which the history of the Roman province teaches us even better to know, this most admirable work of art in the grand style, was a beginning, its structure was designed to *prove itself through thousands of years* — to this day there has been nothing built, nor even dreamed of being built, in the same proportion *sub specie aeterni!* — This organization was firm enough to withstand bad emperors; the chance occurrence of persons has nothing to do with such things — *first* principle of all great architecture. But it was not firm enough against the *most corrupt* kind of corruption, against the Christian kind... This stealthy vermin which in night, fog, and ambiguity stole up to every individual and sucked out of each individual the seriousness for *true* things, the instinct for realities in general, this cowardly, effeminate, and sugar-sweet band alienated "souls" from this tremendous edifice step by step — those valuable, those virile-noble natures who found in the cause of Rome their own cause, their own seriousness, their own pride. This creep-sneakery, conventicle secrecy, gloomy concepts like hell, like sacrifice of the innocent, like *unio mystica* in the drinking of blood, above all the slowly stirred-up fire of revenge, of chandala revenge — *that* became master of Rome, the same sort of religion that in its pre-existing form Epicurus had already made war on. One should read Lucretius in order to see *what* Epicurus opposed: *not* paganism but "Christianity," by which I mean the corruption of the soul through the concept of guilt, penalty, and immortality. — He opposed the *subterranean* cults, the whole of latent Christianity — to deny immortality was already at that time an actual *redemption.* — And Epicurus would have triumphed, every respectable mind in the Roman Empire was Epicurean: *then Paul appeared...* Paul, chandala hatred against Rome, against "the world," become flesh, become genius, the Jew, the *wandering* Jew *par excellence...* What he divined was how with the help of the small sectarian Christian movement apart from Judaism one could ignite a "world conflagration," how with the symbol of "God on the Cross" one could sum up everything at the bottom, everything secretly rebellious, the entire inheritance of anarchistic activity in the empire, turning it into a tremendous power. "Salvation is of the Jews." — Christianity as a formula for outbidding the subterranean cults of all kinds, those of Osiris, of the Great Mother, of Mithras, for example — *and* for summing them up: the genius of Paul consists in this insight. His instinct in this was so sure that he took the ideas with which these chandala religions managed to fascinate, and with unsparing violence to the truth, he placed them in the mouth of his invention the "Savior," and not only in his mouth — having *made* out of him something that even a Mithras priest could understand... This was his vision on the road to Damascus: he grasped that he *needed* the belief in immortality to devalue "the world," that the concept of "hell" would be master even of Rome — that with the "beyond" one *kills life...* Nihilist and Christian: that rhymes together, that doesn't only rhyme together...

59

That entire labor of the ancient world *in vain*: I have no words to express my feeling over something so atrocious. — And considering that its labor was preliminary labor, that the foundation for a labor of millennia had just been laid with granite self-confidence, the entire *meaning* of the ancient world in vain!... Wherefore Greeks? Wherefore Romans? — All the prerequisites for a learned culture, all the scientific methods, were already there, the great, the incomparable art of reading well had already been established — this prerequisite for a cultural tradition, for a unity of knowledge; natural science, in union with mathematics and mechanics, was on the best of all paths — the *sense for facts*, the last and most valuable of all the senses, had its schools, its already centuries old tradition! Is this understood? Everything *essential* had been discovered in order to set the work into motion — the methods, one must repeat it ten times, *are* the essential thing, also that which is opposed the longest by laziness and custom. What we have won back for ourselves today with inexpressible self-mastery — for we all still have the bad instincts, the Christian ones, somewhere in our bodies — the free view of reality, the careful hand, patience and seriousness in the smallest thing, the whole *integrity of knowledge* — they were already there! Already more than two thousand years ago! *And*, in addition, good, fine taste and tact! *Not* as brain training! *Not* as "German" education in company with loutish manners! But as body, as gesture, as instinct — as reality, in a word... *All in vain!* Overnight nothing but a memory! — Greeks! Romans! The nobility of instinct, of taste, the methodical investigation, the genius for organization and administration, the faith in, the *will* to a future for man, the great Yes to all things, visible as the *imperium Romanum*, visible to all senses, the grand style not merely art but turned into reality, truth, *life*... And not overwhelmed by a natural event overnight! Not trampled down by Teutons and other clodhoppers! But ruined by crafty, sneaky, invisible, anemic vampires! Not vanquished — just sucked dry! ... Hidden vengefulness, petty envy become *master*! Everything wretched, suffering from itself, afflicted with bad feelings, the whole ghetto-world of the soul suddenly *on top!* — — One need only read some Christian rabble-rouser such as Saint Augustine to see, to *smell*, what kind of unsavory fellows came to the top thereby. One would be deceiving oneself utterly if one presupposed any lack of intelligence among the leaders of the Christian movement — oh, they are clever, clever to the point of holiness, the se Church fathers! What they lack is something quite different. Nature has slighted them — she forgot to give then a modest dowry of respectable, of reasonable, of clean instincts... Between us, they are not even men... If Islam despises Christianity, it is a thousand times right in doing so: Islam presupposes men...

60

Christianity made us lose the harvest of the ancient world, later it made us lose again the harvest of the culture of *Islam*. The wonderful Moorish cultural world of Spain, more closely related to *us* at bottom, speaking more to our sense and taste than Rome and Greece, was *trampled down* (— I do not say by what kind of feet —), why? Because it owed its origin to noble, to manly instincts, because it said yes to life even with the rare and refined treasures of Moorish life!... The Crusaders later did battle with something it would have suited them better to lie down in the dust before — a culture compared with which even our nineteenth century might seem very poor, very "late." — Of course, they wanted booty: The Orient was rich... One should be impartial though! The Crusades — higher piracy, nothing more! The German nobility, Viking nobility really, was in its element there: the Church knew only too well how the German nobility could be *had*... German nobility, always the "Switzers" of the Church, always in the service of all the bad instincts of the Church — but *well paid*... That precisely with the help of German swords, German blood and guts, the Church has carried out its war of deadly enmity against everything noble on earth! There are a host of painful questions at this point. The German nobility is nearly *absent* in the history of higher culture: one can guess the reason... Christianity, alcohol — the two *great* means of corruption... In itself there really should not be a choice with respect to Islam and Christianity, as little as with respect to an Arab and a Jew. The decision has been made: no one is free to still choose here. Either one *is* a chandala, or one is *not*... "War to the knife with Rome! Peace, friendship with Islam": so felt, so *did* that great free spirit, that genius among German emperors, Frederick II. What? must a German first be a genius, first be a free spirit, before he can have *decent* feelings? I do not see how a German could even have *Christian* feelings...

61

Here it is necessary to touch on a memory a hundred times more painful for Germans. The Germans caused the loss of the last great cultural harvest there was for Europe to bring home — that of the *Renaissance.* Does one understand at last, does one *want* to understand, *what* the Renaissance was? The *revaluation of the Christian values,* the attempt, undertaken with all means, with all instincts, with every bit of genius, to bring about the victory of the *opposing* values, the *noble* values... Hitherto there has only been *this* great war, hitherto there has been no more decisive formulation of a question than that posed by the Renaissance — *my* question is its question — : there also has never been a straighter, sharper, more fundamental form of *attack* launched on the entire front and at the center! To attack at the decisive point, at the seat of Christianity itself, to place the *noble* values on the throne there, I mean to say, to bring them into the instincts, into the deepest needs and desires of those who sit there ... I see the possibility before me of a completely unearthly enchantment and color-allurement — it seems to me that it shimmers in all the shudders of refined beauty, that there is an art at work in it so divine, so devilishly-divine, that one searches through millennia in vain for a second such possibility; I see a spectacle so ingenious and so surprisingly paradoxical at the same time that all the gods of Olympus would have had cause for immortal laughter — Cesare Borgia as Pope ... Am I understood? ... *that* would have been the triumph which I alone desire today — : with that Christianity would have been abolished! — What happened? A German monk, Luther, came to Rome. This monk, with all the vindictive instincts of a failed priest in his body, rebelled in Rome *against* the Renaissance ... Instead of understanding with the deepest gratitude the tremendous event which had taken place, the overcoming of Christianity at its seat — , his hatred understood only how to draw its nourishment from the spectacle. A religious man thinks only of himself. — Luther saw the *corruption* of the *Papacy*, while precisely the opposite was right there at hand: the old corruption, the *peccatum originale,* Christianity *no* longer sat on the Papal chair! But life instead! The triumph of life! The great Yes to all high, fair, daring things! ... and Luther *restored the Church*: he attacked it... The Renaissance — an event without meaning, a great In-vain! — Ah these Germans, what they have already cost us! In-vain — that has always been the *work* of the Germans. — The Reformation; Leibniz; Kant and the so-called German philosophy; the Wars of "Liberation," the Reich — each time an In-vain for something already there, for something *irretrievable* ... They are my enemies, I confess it, these Germans: I despise in them every kind of concept and value uncleanliness, every kind of cowardice before every honest Yes and No. For almost a thousand years they have mussed up and messed up everything they laid their hands on, they have on their conscience everything half-hearted — three-eighths-hearted! — from which Europe is sick — they also have on their conscience the uncleanest kind of Christianity there is, the most incurable, the most irrefutable: Protestantism ... If we are not finished with Christianity, the *Germans* will be to blame ...

62

— With this I am at the end and pronounce my judgment. I condemn Christianity; I raise against the Christian Church the most terrible accusation that any accuser has ever uttered. To me it is the highest of all conceivable forms of corruption, it has had the will to the last corruption possible. The Christian Church has left nothing untouched by its depravity; out of every value it has made an unvalue, out of every truth a lie out of every act of uprightness a vileness of the soul. People still dare to talk to me of its "humanitarian" blessings! To *abolish* any state of distress ran counter to its deepest advantage: it fed on states of distress, it *created* states of distress, in order to perpetuate *itself* ... The worm of sin, for example: it was the Church that first enriched mankind with this state of distress! — The "equality of souls before God," this falsehood, this *pretext* for the *rancune* of all the low-minded, this concept explosive which eventually became revolution, modern idea, and the principle of the decline of the entire social order — is *Christian* dynamite ... "Humanitarian" blessings of Christianity! To cultivate out of *humanitas* a self-contradiction, an art of self-desecration, a will to untruth at any price, an ill-will, a contempt for all good and honest instincts! These to me are the blessings of Christianity! — Parasitism as the *sole* practice of the Church; with its ideal of greensickness, of holiness draining all blood, all love, all hope for life; the beyond as a will to the denial of all reality; the Cross as the sign of recognition for the most subterranean conspiracy there has ever been — against health, beauty, successfulness, bravery, intellect, *goodness* of soul, *against life itself...*

This eternal accusation against Christianity I will write on all walls, wherever there are walls — I have letters to make even the blind see ... I call Christianity the *one* great curse, the *one* great innermost depravity, the *one* great instinct of revenge for which no means is poisonous, stealthy, subterranean, *small* enough — I call it the *one* immortal blemish on mankind ...

And one reckons, *time* from the dies *nefastus* on which this disaster began — from the *first* day of Christianity! *Why not rather from its last? — From today? —*

Revaluation of all values!